*Momma Always Said* **PIGS IS PIGS** *and*
# Folks is Folks

## Reminiscing about
## Family, Friends and Food

# Raleigh McDonald Hussung

# Dedication

I Dedicate This Book With Love To...The Man Upstairs and Four of His Angels—Momma, Mana, Grandmother and Peggy, from Raleigh,...To Daddy from Miss Priss,...To Bo, Michael and John from Mom,...To B, M, & J at NEW—you showed me that it would and could run without me and inspite of me,...To B from R,...To Ann and Judy from "Sis," ...To Anne and Big Buck from your "favorite and only daughter-in-law,"...and, ...To all of my friends from Rawls.

A special note to all who are mentioned in this book—I hope that I have pleased, not displeased. I wrote what I knew and remembered; I wrote with love and respect for each of you. I hope you will smile and chuckle along with me. I have had an absolute ball!! Thanks for the ride!!!

Library of Congress Number: 97-092373
ISBN: 0-9658827-0-5

Designed, Edited and Manufactured by
Favorite Recipes® Press
an imprint of

FRP

P.O. Box 305142, Nashville, Tennessee 37230
800-358-0560

Art Director: Steve Newman
Cover and Production Design: Bill Kersey
Project Manager: Georgia Brazil

Manufactured in the United States of America
First Printing: 1997  10,000 copies

# Contents

# *Preface*

### *The Promise That Became This Cookbook*

I made a promise to my mother that you need to know about. Why? Because you need to understand why I felt compelled—driven, actually—to add one more cookbook to the millions already out there! And you need to know that my husband, Buck, and I have three sons, no daughters. We do have two great daughters-in-law and will be soon be gaining a third one. We also have four incredibly neat grandchildren, you will understand later...!

Momma began telling me "to write it down" as early as 1962. I had absolutely no idea what she meant, but, I would always respond that I would, if she would only tell me what she wanted me to write about. The last time she told me was just before she died in 1992. This time she asked me to "promise" to write it down. I promised. I still didn't have the foggiest idea what she meant so I didn't really think too much about it. Until about a year and a half ago..., I was watching television and out of curiosity I called one of those psychic networks (you know...they advertise all the time!) and the psychic I reached told me that I was going to write a book! Well, needless to say, I was surprised and somewhat puzzled! I still didn't dwell much on it and I didn't tell anyone about the call except my husband, Buck, when the telephone bill arrived! And then, I felt silly about even making the call. I certainly wasn't going to mention what she had said about the book. I will admit that I did have a hard time dismissing that the psychic and Momma had both mentioned "writing a book." It had to be a coincidence. I had almost convinced myself that I really was being silly. I almost did—until...this past summer—Buck and I were at some friends' house having dinner and talking about things each of us had done that the others present might think silly if they knew about it. I mentioned the psychic network call and told them what the psychic had told me. Well, they didn't think it was silly at all.

They thought that was an intriguing idea. Then, they all asked, "What would you write about?" I said that I had said the exact thing many times to my mother when she told me that I would write a book. At this they all asked, "Your mother told you the same thing that the psychic did?" I nodded. They were in shock! Anyway, I seriously began to think about the book and thought, why not!...But what kind of book?...For many years I had been told by friends and family that I should either start a catering company, open a restaurant, or at least write a cookbook. None of these ideas did much for me at the times they were mentioned; I always responded that it would take all the fun out of cooking! I should have remembered "never say never," because last Fall, something occurred that changed my mind and made me positively sure that the book I promised to write was a cookbook—this cookbook!

Early in November last year, I was asked by a friend–Anne Byrne Whitaker, who writes about food and gardening for *The Tennessean,* the morning newspaper in Nashville, to conduct a cooking class for four young women who were graduate students at Vanderbilt University, not going home for Thanksgiving, and had never cooked a turkey. This would be a feature article in *The Tennessean* two weeks before Thanksgiving. It sounded like a fun Sunday thing to do, so I agreed! It was fun and they did learn how to cook a whole turkey dinner! Of course, my turkey recipe was Momma's and Mana's—and it has never produced anything but an incredible bird—stuffed with a wonderful dressing and baked until perfectly golden brown…and always juicy! It was perfect this time too! The article was great and even though I had a couple of weeks until turkey day, I was inspired and began to plan the dinner. Of course, including all of the traditional elements: turkey, dressing, wild rice, gravy, scalloped oysters, sweet potatoes, green beans, and cranberry sauce. The pies—pumpkin, mince, and pecan; maybe this year I'd make a chocolate or an apple one too! Then it hit me…I was planning my dinner exactly like the ones I had eaten all my life!…I had eaten…my traditions!…Yikes, I thought…my daughters-in-law would do as I had—they would use their families' traditions; my granddaughter would use her mother's.

That's simply the way it has always been, especially in the South. They might incorporate some of my recipes; but, I thought as I began to really freak out, no one will cook turkey and dressing the way I do, the way I was taught to do, when I'm gone—all my teachers will be up there with me!!…The light bulb went on over my head! The bell gonged! "Write it down" became clear!…

You see, Momma "knew things"—she could actually tell you things that were going to happen before they happened. It was more than intuition or a "sixth sense," it was a God-given gift. She always explained it as a gift that one person in every generation of her mother's family had always had, and would continue to have until God chose not to give it. She said Mana didn't have it, but Mana's sister—"Sister" had been the one who had it. So, knowing this about Momma, it was clear to me that she knew back in 1962, before I was married, before I had even met my future husband, that I wouldn't have a daughter to pass all the things on to that had been passed on to me! Clearly, she meant that it was up to me to write it down so that they wouldn't be lost.

And so, I'm keeping my promise to Momma. I am writing it down, it won't be lost, I will pass it on. Also, I have converted all of the "pinches," "dashes," and other non-measurements to easily followed directions. Please feel free to adjust these seasoning amounts for your personal tastes; a bit more or less won't hurt a thing. I always adjust, I've never known a good cook who didn't.

February, 1997

# What is Southern Cooking?

"Let me see," said that old blind Southern gentlemen. And, he even knew he couldn't see when he said it!...Well, it was right then that I said, "Let me see!"...And, this is what I see the answer to be...

...A melding of cuisines from as far away as Europe and Africa, and as close as South America and the Caribbean is one answer.

And..., the cuisine of the South is another.

All of these are right; but, there's a whole lot more to it. To find out how much more, you have to ask a Southern Cook.

Ask, and you will hear about the recipes and traditions which were, and still are, passed down from one generation to the next. You will hear the little stories that are as much a part of the traditions as the recipes are. All of those things that were rarely written down, always "taught." Usually by mothers to daughters. And almost always considered "Family Secrets!" I am a Southern Cook, and I am going to explain what I know about Southern Cooking by sharing "Family Secrets" with a lot of little stories with you. These are recipes passed on to me by my mother, "Momma," her mother, "Mana," my father's mother, "Grandmother," and a terrific cook named Peggy. There are recipes from my husband, Buck, and his family. There are some from friends. There are "old" old ones, "old" new ones, and even a few "new" new ones. Recipes and stories, ...all were "secrets" — until now.

# Backgrounds, Histories and
# Some Family Stories

# *The Bells—*
# *My Mother's Family*

- *Maria Alberta Drake Bell (Momma's Mother), "Alberta" — "Mana"*
- *John Mills Bell (Momma's Father), "John" — "Boppa"*
- *Maria Alberta Drake Bell McDonald, "Berta" — Momma*
- *Ann Finch Bell Haynes, "Ann"*

# *The McDonalds—*
# *My Father's Family*

- *Mabel Morris McDonald (Daddy's Mother), "Mabel" — "Grandmother"*
- *Paul McDonald, M.D. (Daddy's Father), "Paul" — "Grandfather"*
- *Harold Paul McDonald, "Harold"*
- *Mabel Eleanor McDonald Elsas Storza, "Eleanor"*
- *Lois Carolyn McDonald Jorgenson, "Lois"*
- *Allen Pierce McDonald, "Pierce"*
- *Morris Irwin McDonald, "Morris" (Daddy)*
- *James Benteen McDonald, "Benteen"*
  *and, me–Raleigh Ann McDonald Hussung, "Raleigh" — "Sis" — "Rawls"*

# *The Hussungs—*
# *My Husband Buck's Family*

- *Elizabeth Lawrence Hussung (Buck's Mother), "Anne"*
- *M.V. Hussung, Sr. (Buck's Father), "Big Buck"*
- *Mamie Davis Davis (Buck's Great-Great-Aunt), "Aunt Mamie"*
- *Mae Montgomery (Buck's Great-Aunt), "Mae"*
- *Aileen Montgomery Lawrence (Buck's Grandmother), "Ene"*
- *M.V. Hussung, Jr. (My Husband), "Buck"*
- *Iva Hussung (Big Buck's Mother), "Grandma"*

# The Bells—My Mother's Family

Momma's mother and father, Albert and John Mills Bell, moved to Atlanta from Nashville after they married in 1915. Mana was born in Riverside, California; her mother (my great-grandmother, Annie Augusta Finch Drake) was originally from Nashville and had moved to California when she married John Drake who was a Californian. The Drakes were a well-to-do family in Riverside — owning a business there — Drake's Books — and large homes and land — "pillars of the community." Mana and her older sister, "Sister" (actually — Annie Augusta Drake), were born there and lived there with their parents until John Drake "fell dead in the street." I was told that he landed more or less in the gutter that ran beside the street. Anyway, it seems that was where he was found — the morning after a night of "celebrating." After his death, Annie (my great-grandmother), Mana, and Sister moved back to Nashville to be close to Annie's family. Annie did remain very close to the Drakes, and took her girls to visit them in California often. In later years, Mana would take Momma and Ann (Momma's sister) to "visit" for most of every summer. When Momma and Ann were little, they would take the train or Boppa would drive them. Then, when they were older they would take a cruise through the Panama Canal and disembark in California. Quite FUN! Momma said that she and Ann and Mana were invited to private parties and such, and they met stars like Clark Gable and Douglas Fairbanks. Momma loved to tell stories about their trips to California — stories about "Cousin Gene," "Cousin Frances," Rivers, "Nuge" and Felice, and "Nuge" and Else. I never met them, but felt like I knew them!

Getting back to where I got a little sidetracked — Mana, Sister, and their mother moved to Nashville, Tennessee, to be near "family," Mana met a young Nashville man named John Mills Bell, and, after courting for the proper amount of time, married him. John Mills Bell (Boppa) was born in Nashville. His Grandfather, James Bell, had settled in south Davidson County, Tennessee, in 1820. He moved his family from South Carolina, through Georgia and Alabama, to Tennessee. He was one of the early settlers in this area which is now Brentwood. He was a farmer and a blacksmith. Actually, Bell Road in southern Davidson County was so named because it went to the Bell Farm. Inserting a little trivia here — I have always thought it to be rather unusual that I would come to Nashville to attend Vanderbilt, marry a "Nashville boy," and live in Nashville. It's sort of a "full circle" back to my grandparents' roots; and, my home in southern Davidson County is on property that could have belonged to my great-great-grandfather! The property was sold in the early 1900s and all of my grandfather's family moved to the Goodlettsville area. There's no one left from either my grandfather's or grandmother's families. I have done some research at the Tennessee State Archives and have been able to trace at least this far into the history of my grandfather's family in Tennessee. Luckily, I completed this bit of research while Momma was alive and she was able to help. Momma did say we were related to the Bells of "Bell Witch Fame." I've got more "digging" to do to prove that. However…, As I have said, Momma did have that "gift," so…! End of trivia — at least for now.

Continuing on, Mana and Boppa lived in Atlanta — Momma was three years older. Momma was the "wild one" or the risk-taker. She would do just about anything "on a dare." And she was always getting Ann in trouble! Ann would "tattle" on Momma, Momma would threaten to kill Ann, and Mana would referee! There was always a little jealousy between

Momma and Ann—Momma didn't like the idea that she had to share her Mother and Father with somebody else, especially a little sister that nobody even asked her if she wanted! They were sisters, they were friends, just not best friends.

Ann said that she and Momma did laugh and have lots of good times as they got older—they both had incredible great senses of humor! That's certainly the truth! And it's certainly the truth that they grew up to be beautiful redheads—known in Atlanta as "the beautiful Bell girls." Momma's hair was a very deep, rich auburn shade, and Ann's was a lighter, more golden red. They were two of the most popular girls in Atlanta—Momma said that Sunday afternoons when the boys "would come to call," there would always be at least 10 of them in the front parlor—Every Sunday! Before each of them married, Momma said there were boys who actually swore they would kill themselves—of course they didn't and these boys did find happiness with others!

…Time for a little trivia here—I remember one time, when I was in high school, I was upset because I had just broken up with my boyfriend and I was sure that my life just wouldn't go on! Teenagers are a dramatic and rather emotional group! Anyway, Momma looked at me, smiled, and, with that incredible southern drawl she had, said "Sweetheart, men are just like streetcars—there will be another one along in a few minutes; and if you miss that one, there will be another right after!" In other words, it's not the end of the world! More trivia,…About the southern drawl: Mana, Momma, and Ann all talked with a drawl that poured out like slow molasses. When Momma would call me, I swear it took her forever to say "Raleigh"—she

> "Sweetheart, men are just like streetcars—there will be another one along in a few minutes; and if you miss that one, there will be another right after!"

would draw that one word out forever! There are some folks who think I sound a lot like her

maybe it's something in the genes, because my cousin Judy, Ann's daughter, sure does sound like Ann!…Anyway, Momma and Ann both married Atlanta boys. Momma married Morris Irwin McDonald (Daddy) in 1941. Ann and James Augustus Haynes married in 1942. At first, Daddy worked for the Telephone Company. After Uncle Jimmy came home from serving in World War II, Daddy and Uncle Jimmy joined Boppa's company—the John M. Bell Co. Inc.—which was a textile waste company in the early 1950s. Momma and Daddy had three children: Johnny, me, and Morris, Jr. Ann and Uncle Jimmy had Judy and "Gus" (Jimmy Jr.).

Boppa died in 1957, Mana in 1962, Uncle Jimmy in 1985, and Momma in 1992—there's a real weird almost "twilight zone" connection concerning the dates they died on—Momma died on the 8th, Boppa on the 9th, Uncle Jimmy on the 10th, and Mana on the 11th. Different years and months, but, still a little eerie. When Uncle Jimmy died on the 10th, Momma said that she would be the next to "go" and it would be on either the 8th or the 12th. She was right, as usual. Ann swears that when she "goes" it will be either on the 7th or 12th…!

Anyway, Ann lives in Oregon now—which is about a world away from Atlanta. I do love talking with her, she knows the greatest jokes! As a matter of fact, Daddy is the only one still in Atlanta.

# The McDonalds — My Father's Family

Mabel Lee Morris and Paul McDonald, Daddy's parents, lived in Georgia all of their lives. They married in Atlanta in 1902. They lived on a hill in a big white Victorian home on Bolton Road just outside Atlanta. Grandfather was a doctor and his office was in the house. I remember even on holidays, like Christmas or Easter, there would be patients sitting on the big swing seat outside his office. All waiting to see "Dr. Paul." He was a family doctor — who took care of everything — from birth to death. He probably delivered and took care of at least two generations of people in his 60 years of practice. All of the people in and around Bolton came to him. He was also the physician for the Fulton County Prison work crews — known as "chain gangs." Of course Grandfather took care of his own family. He would come to our house when we children were sick; and after assessing what was wrong — if he thought we needed one — give us a shot of penicillin with what I was sure was the biggest hypodermic syringe I had ever seen! He always left a bottle of "pink medicine." This was a concoction — of his own invention — that would cure any cold, flu, fever, or cough you ever had. Magic Stuff! He would pour a little of this, and drop of that, adding secret things that were contained in all of those bottles that were in the sides of his old black leather medicine bag into a single bottle that he would leave, telling Momma to be sure to "give it to us every four hours." I was always fascinated when he mixed it up and it always worked. Sure wish I had a recipe for that! A little bit of trivia — Grandfather made a medicine that was the exact duplicate of campo-phenique, only he invented his way before campo-phenique was invented. He gave this to patients for cuts, abrasions, skin infections, etc., and I guess this recipe died with him too. Oh well. Anyway, while Grandfather was busy curing people, Grandmother was raising their six children and keeping the home fires burning bright. The property on Bolton Road had, in addition to the big house, some small fields that were planted with vegetables, and a small house occupied by the family that helped Grandmother tend to the running of things. AND, Grandfather had his own gasoline pump! By the time I was old enough to notice it, it wasn't used anymore. I'm sure he only had it because he was a doctor in a rural area of Atlanta, and he took care of the prisoners at the prison. I guess it was there so he wouldn't ever be without gas, and so he could get anywhere he needed to be and at any time. I still think it was neat!

The house and land were sold after Grandmother died in 1972; so, what was there is only a memory now — and, office buildings!

Grandmother and Grandfather expected each of their children to do well at whatever they chose to do. They wouldn't accept anything but the best from them. Their children grew up to be independent, dedicated, and fiercely loyal people — all were successes in life. They had several children — six lived to adulthood — Harold, Eleanor, Lois, Pierce, Morris (Daddy), and Benteen. All, except Benteen, lived and raised their families in Atlanta.

Uncle Harold was the first child and first son. He was a well known urologist. He and Aunt Callie had two sons: Harold, Jr. and Larry. Both of them were urologists, too. However, Larry gave up his practice, got involved in politics, ran for the U.S. Congress from Georgia, and won. He died in 1983. He was on the Korean Airlines Plane that was shot down for "drifting" into the wrong place at the wrong time! His constituents in Cobb County dedicated the section of I-75 that goes through Cobb County to his memory.

Aunt Eleanor was the first daughter, third child, and our Auntie Mame! She was first married to Uncle Billy (William Elsas). He died from a heart attack. Their home in Atlanta, Moccasin Hollow, sat on over 60 acres of land. They had horses, stables, beautiful pastures, and an incredible house that was built to overlook the wetlands where Aunt Eleanor killed the water moccasins! She put on waders, and with a sawed-off shotgun, marched through the creeks and wetlands that were on their property, killing every water moccasin she saw! She later planted these wet areas with water lilies and other water plants to create beautiful vistas to look at from the house. She played the piano. As a matter of fact, all six children played a musical instrument — Daddy played the trombone! She and Uncle Billy were among the founders of the Shakerag Hounds fox hunting organization in Atlanta. She and her second husband, Uncle Francis (Francis Storza), provided the funds needed to establish the "Storza Woods" area at the Atlanta Botanical Gardens. She and Uncle Francis married a few years after Uncle Billy died.

Aunt Lois is the second girl and third child. She taught elementary school in Atlanta. She married Matt Jorgenson and they had three daughters: Carolyn, Maren, and Anna. Uncle Matt was an architect. His projects included Crawford Long Hospital in Atlanta, and St. Thomas Hospital and Baptist Hospital in Nashville. Aunt Lois is my godmother and a "shoulder" when I need one. A special lady.

*Momma said that when she met Daddy for the first time, she thought he was the "best looking thing on two legs" she had ever seen!*

Uncle Pierce was the fifth child and third son. He was a dentist. He was married to Adelaide Porter and they had three sons: Allen, Bobby, and Paul. Aunt Adelaide was an artist, and she and Uncle Pierce were involved in the arts in Atlanta. They were among the members of the Atlanta Art Society who were killed in 1962 at Orly Airport, in Paris, when their plane crashed on takeoff. Everyone I knew had either a relative that perished, or knew someone who did. It was a very sad time for Atlanta and for us.

My Father, Morris, was the sixth child and fourth son. He was the athlete in the family. When he was in high school, he was first-string quarterback on the football team, the center for the basketball team, pitcher on the baseball team, and won the Fulton County championship in tennis — doubles — 18 and under — when he was 18. He went to Darlington College on a basketball scholarship, transferred to the University of Georgia, and played basketball there. At 6 feet 3½ inches, he was the tallest man on the team! He always looked bigger than that to me and my brothers — especially when he was mad!

All four McDonald boys were handsome, but everybody said that Daddy was the best looking. Momma said that when she met him for the first time, she thought he was the "best looking thing on two legs" she had ever seen!

Daddy and Momma married in 1941. Daddy always said that the reason he married Momma was her beautiful red hair. Well,...Momma got real mad at Daddy in 1978 and bleached that beautiful red hair. She remained a blonde until she died in 1992. Momma was like that sometimes. Daddy always says she was a maverick; and, if she loved you, you knew it; and if she didn't like you — you knew that too. One of her favorite sayings was, "Pigs is Pigs, and Folks is Folks." Momma could make you laugh — she had a great sense of humor — she and Daddy had a good time — they were married for 51 years! It's for sure he never knew quite what to expect next — life with Momma was never dull!

Uncle Benteen was the seventh child and fifth son. He was the "baby" in this family of independent individuals. I'm sure he had to fight all the time just to be heard! Maybe that's why he moved to Newport, Tennessee! He married Eunice Holt and they have a daughter, Jama.

# A Little About Me — Raleigh Ann McDonald Hussung

As I have said, all six McDonald children were taught to be strong, independent individuals — they were taught to succeed. Each of them chose a strong, independent person to marry.

I am the middle child and only girl born to two of the most independent of the group! Being the only girl wasn't really a plus factor where I was concerned — it just meant I had to try a little harder than my brothers, who were always ganging up on me. The only time I had the advantage over them was the time I broke my elbow and had a monster of a cast that I could use as a weapon. I'm a lot like both Momma and Daddy. I have always been a maverick and a loner. I am fiercely hardheaded and stubborn. I don't and won't take "no" for an answer. I believe that right is right and wrong is wrong and there's not too much in between.

I am an unconditional friend to my friends and would do anything for those I love. I am opinioniated but...diplomatic. I am terrible at sports — I don't like to sweat! I can be a wild and crazy woman, but...always a lady! I don't tolerate cruelty and meanness in anyone — or from anyone! I love to create "lemonade from lemons" and I believe that, with God's help, there's very little I can't accomplish. If "it" can be done, I'll find a way. I can be maddeningly exasperating sometimes; thank goodness I married someone who is as strong as I am! He can be just as exasperating...sometimes!!

I am a very lucky lady — my brothers and I grew up with the guidance and help of a Mother and Father who loved us and taught us, by example, to be the very best we were capable of being — that Life is the real thing — "not a dress rehearsal."

P.S. My nicknames: "Sis" is what Momma, Mana, and Ann always called me. Daddy called me "Miss Priss." "Rawls" is a nickname given me a few years ago by a friend, and is what my grandchildren and close friends call me. I thought it would be a neat "Nom de Plume"!!

# *The Hussungs —*
# *My Husband Buck's Family*

Buck's Mother, Anne, was born in Nashville and has lived here all her life. She and her sister, Dot, were raised by three women who were well ahead of their times! Through no fault of their own, Aunt Mamie, Ene, and Mae were forced to be the bread winners when it wasn't "chic" for women to work. And they were all successful — at their jobs and raising Anne and Dot!!

Buck's Father, a.k.a. Buck — that's why I call him "Big Buck" — is from Illinois. He was one of six children born to Iva and William Hussung. He and Anne met and married in Nashville and live here now.

They have two children, Buck and his sister, Kerry. Kerry lives in Nashville and is married to Tom Harrison.

Buck and I met while we were students at Vanderbilt. We married in 1963 and we have lived in Nashville the whole time we have been married, except for three years — 1976 to 1979 — when we lived in Greenville, South Carolina. We have three sons: Bo (M.V., III), Michael, and John.

Buck and I own National Embroidery Works, Inc. — a contract embroidery business. Michael and John work with us; Bo works for a mortgage company.

*I'm blessed with a wonderful family, great friends, and I'm enjoying the ride!!*

# My Family
# Favorite Recipes

# My Family Favorites

Momma made the most delicious vegetable soup, potato salad, lumpy oatmeal, and cocoa fudge in the world. Her mother, Mana, made the best pimento cheese and blue cheese dip/spread, fruitcake, and "special" Coca-Cola ice cream float ever! My father's mother, Grandmother, made Brunswick stew that had 'em lining up for miles—ditto for her creamed corn, turkey hash, and fried chicken. Thank heaven I have the recipes, because they're further away than even AT&T can "reach" and I'm not even sure phones are allowed up there!

# ~≈ Momma's Vegetable Soup ≈~

### *This recipe can be doubled easily.*

| | |
|---|---|
| 2 large and meaty beef soup bones | 1 small head of cabbage, chopped fine |
| salt and pepper to taste | 1 (28-ounce) can of tomatoes, chopped and added with juice |
| 1 bunch of celery, diced | 1 (14-ounce) bottle of ketchup |
| 1 large onion, diced | Sometimes she would add a package of frozen lima beans. |
| 4 or 5 carrots, sliced | |

Place the beef bones in a stockpot and cover the bones with water. Place on the stove and cook for about 30 minutes, skimming any foamy residue with a slotted spoon. Add salt and pepper to taste at this point. Add diced celery, diced onion, sliced carrots, and the chopped cabbage. Simmer over low heat for 1 hour. Add the chopped tomatoes and their juice. Cook another hour. Add one 14-ounce bottle of ketchup—Momma used Del Monte or Stokleys. Let simmer for at least 30 minutes and check seasonings before adding additional salt and pepper to taste.

**Note:** This soup can be refrigerated and reheated for a week's worth of dinners. It does get thicker and can be thinned with water. It also freezes beautifully!

## Rawls' ~≈ Additions

• *Instead of using soup bones, I buy a small chuck roast and remove the visible fat and cut it into small bite-sized pieces.*

• *I add these additional vegetables: 1 package each of frozen green peas, green beans, corn, and lima beans.*

*Neither Momma nor I ever add potatoes; because, when the soup is reheated after refrigerating, the potatoes tend to get very mealy.*

## ᔓ Rawls' Additions

• *I reduce the sweet pickles to 2 and add 2 diced dill pickles. I also add ¹/₂ cup sliced pimento-stuffed green olives. I add equal amounts of sweet pickle juice and dill pickle juice to make up the ¹/₄ cup of sweet pickle juice called for in Momma's recipe.*

• *Momma used Kraft real mayonnaise; I do, too. You can use salad dressing instead of the real mayonnaise; but the potato salad will be sweeter. Here again, I recommend Kraft.*

## ᔓ Momma's Potato Salad ᔓ

### *This recipe makes a large mixing bowl full.*

| | |
|---|---|
| 6 large Idaho baking potatoes boiled in their jackets, cooled, peeled, and cut into medium dice | 3 sweet pickles, diced |
| | ¹/₄ cup sweet pickle juice |
| | mayonnaise to moisten (about ¹/₂ to ³/₄ cup) |
| 4 large eggs, hard-boiled and chopped | 1 tablespoon Durkees sauce |
| 6 ribs celery, thinly sliced | salt and pepper to taste |

Put the potatoes and eggs into a large mixing bowl; add the sliced celery and the sweet pickles. Pour ¹/₄ cup sweet pickle juice over everything. Mix the mayonnaise with the Durkees sauce and pour over the salad. Mix with hands, taste, and add salt and pepper to taste. Chill well before serving.

*The addition of the Durkees sauce gives the salad a little tang! Durkees sauce is one ingredient I would not be without in my kitchen.*

## ᔓ Momma's Cocoa Fudge ᔓ

### *This is very old-fashioned fudge. I think it is delicious.*

| | |
|---|---|
| 3 cups sugar | ¹/₄ teaspoon salt |
| 6 tablespoons of Hershey's unsweetened cocoa powder | ³/₄ cup whole milk |
| | 1 teaspoon pure vanilla extract |
| 2 tablespoons white corn syrup | ¹/₂ stick butter |

Pour sugar, cocoa, corn syrup, salt, and milk in the saucepan. Bring to the boil and cook until a soft ball forms when a small amount is dipped into cold water. At this point add the vanilla, stir, and when it comes back up to the boil remove from the heat and add the butter. Beat by hand until all of the butter is incorporated—be careful not to splatter because it is very hot! Immediately pour into a buttered 9-inch pan. Let cool and cut into squares.

# Some Other Things Momma Would
## Stir Up From Time To Time:

### Momma's Peanut Butter Bacon Bread

Spread peanut butter on white bread, place two strips of bacon on top of the peanut butter, and broil until the bacon is cooked. Watch carefully to be sure the peanut butter doesn't get too brown. This works best when the pan used is placed low in the oven, not close to the broiler element.

### Momma's Cheese Rolls

Place a slice of either American or Swiss cheese on a slice of bread and roll up. Wrap a slice of bacon around the roll and secure with a toothpick. Bake in a 400-degree oven, turning 2 or 3 times until brown. Serve as a luncheon accompaniment to a salad or as an hors d'oeuvre.

### Momma's Saltine S'Mores

Place a large marshmallow on a saltine cracker and broil until the marshmallow is toasty brown—sort of a s'more without the chocolate and graham crackers!

### Momma's Lumpy Oatmeal

To make "lumpy" oatmeal—cook the oatmeal longer than called for in the directions—it should be like thick paste. Put it, while very hot, in a bowl; sprinkle sugar on it and pour milk over it. Do not mix. Wait until it has cooled enough to eat and enjoy. The milk will be very warm and the oatmeal will be lumpy!

### Momma's Pineapple Cream Cheese Salad

Place a few lettuce leaves on a plate. Put 2 pineapple slices on top of the lettuce. Roll balls of cream cheese and (optional) roll the balls in pecans. Put the balls in the center of each pineapple slice. Mix ½ cup of mayonnaise and 1 tablespoon of Durkees sauce and spoon on the salad. Simply delicious!

# Daddy's Great Grits
## ❧ And Poached Salmon ❧

### Daddy's Great Grits

The secret to making smooth grits is constantly, and I do mean constantly, and gently stirring the boiling water as you pour the grits in. After they are stirred in, turn the heat down to a simmer and cover. Stir them occasionally until they are done. Add the salt, pepper, and butter after they are done.

*Daddy loved to "piddle around" in the kitchen—he taught me how to make great grits and a wonderful poached salmon.*

### Daddy's Poached Salmon

Put 2 sliced limes in the bottom of an oblong pan. Add 3 sliced lemons, a teaspoonful of black peppercorns, an onion—thinly sliced, and 4 or 5 bay leaves. You should have covered the whole bottom of the pan, creating a sort of shell to put the salmon on, so it won't be sitting directly in the poaching liquid as it cooks. Pour white wine over the lemons, etc.—just to barely come to the top of them. Wrap the salmon in cheesecloth, place the salmon directly on the lemons, etc., cover and place on a burner on the stove. Bring the liquid to the boil; immediately turn the heat down to a simmer. Simmer, covered, for 30 minutes. Turn the heat off and let the salmon cool in the pan. Serve either hot or cold with the following sauce.

# Sour Cream
## ❧ Mustard Sauce ❧

*This sauce can be served warm or cold.*

Combine a 16-ounce carton of sour cream with $3/4$ cup Dijon mustard. Add $1/4$ cup chopped fresh parsley and 1 teaspoon of dried tarragon.

## ❧ Daddy's Baked Vidalia Onion ❧

Really a special treat when those sweet Vidalias are in season. And so-o-o-easy! Cut off the bottom of a medium Vidalia onion and core it, making a cone-shaped hole—don't cut all the way through. Then, cut a thin slice off the top of the onion, so it will stand up in the pan. Place the onion in a Pam-sprayed pan. Put a small pat of butter in the hole and fill it with honey—Daddy's favorite is Tupelo Honey. Bake it in a 400-degree oven for 30 minutes. Yum…yum!

# ⇜ Mana's Pimento Cheese ⇝

### *This recipe can easily be doubled or tripled.*

| | |
|---|---|
| **12 ounces Cheddar cheese—** Mana uses hoop cheese | **1 teaspoon pickle juice** mayonnaise—start with ¼ cup |
| **1 small jar pimentos** | **1 teaspoon Durkees sauce** |
| **1 sweet pickle, finely chopped** | salt and pepper to taste |

Grate the cheese on the fine side of a four-sided grater. Put into a mixing bowl. Drain the pimentos and mash into the cheese with a fork. Add the chopped pickle and the teaspoon of pickle juice. Add the mayonnaise, Durkees sauce, and salt and pepper to taste. Mix well with a fork. Use as a spread or stuff into celery.

# ⇜ Mana's Blue Cheese Dip/Spread ⇝

### *Easily doubled and tripled.*

| | |
|---|---|
| **4 ounces blue cheese** | **1 tablespoon (or more)** |
| **8 ounces Philadelphia** cream cheese | **mayonnaise** pepper and salt to taste |

Let the cheeses come to room temperature. Place the cream cheese in a bowl, add a tablespoon of mayonnaise, and blend with a fork until it is the consistency of thick paste, adding a bit more mayonnaise if necessary. Mash the blue cheese with a fork and blend it into the cream cheese mixture. It should be a little lumpy. Add pepper and taste for salt—you may not need any salt; the blue cheese may be salty enough. Chill before serving. Serve on crackers, stuff into celery, or use in a pear or pineapple salad: place a pear half or a pineapple slice on a lettuce leaf and put a dollop of blue cheese dip on top.

---

# Rawls' ⇝ Additions

• *I use 12 ounces extra-sharp white Cheddar, ½ cup shredded Parmesan, ½ cup Feta or Gorgonzola, and 8 ounces mild Cheddar.*

• *I use 2 jars of diced pimentos. I omit the pickles and add 1 more teaspoon of pickle juice instead.*

• *I double the amount of mayonnaise and Durkees sauce. I use an electric hand mixer and end up with a smoother product.*

• *Try this spread on flour tortillas. Roll them up and slice into 1-inch pieces. Great appetizer! Vary also by substituting a can of chopped green chiles for the pimentos. Try substituting 2 tablespoons of finely chopped jalapeños. Try stuffing the mixture into fresh Anaheim chiles and slicing. Use your imagination!*

---

• *It would also be delicious to substitute tomatoes or apples for the pear and the pineapple.*

• *Try spooning room temperature dip on grilled burgers or steak.*

• *Add 8 ounces of sour cream, some dillweed, or chopped parsley and use as a dip for veggies.*

• *Try adding 12 ounces sour cream and an envelope of French's dry onion soup mix. Use as a dip for chips.*

## ❧ Rawls' Additions

*I omit the cherries, add 8 ounces grated sharp white Cheddar, 2 tablespoons dried green onions, 1 tablespoon Lawry's Seasoned Salt, 1 tablespoon Durkees sauce, 1 teaspoon onion powder, and ½ cup chopped pecans or walnuts. Roll this into logs or a ball and then roll in chopped chives. Serve as an hors d'oeuvre with ginger-snaps—unusual and very tasty!*

# Mana's Pineapple ❧ Cream Cheese Spread ❧

### *This can be doubled and tripled easily.*

1 (7-ounce) can of pineapple slices

16 ounces Philadelphia cream cheese, at room temperature

1 tablespoon mayonnaise to soften the cream cheese

6 maraschino cherries, chopped

1 teaspoon Durkees sauce

Drain the pineapple, reserving the juice. With a fork, mash the pineapple coarsely. Place the cheese in a bowl. Add 1 tablespoon of mayonnaise to the cream cheese; mix well with a fork—it will be stiff. Add the pineapple and enough of the juice to make it spreadable; blend well with a fork. Add the maraschino cherries and the Durkees sauce and mix well.

# ❧ Mana's Ice Cream Float ❧

Mana used to make delicious special ice cream floats, with ginger ale instead of Coca-Cola. Why? Momma told me this: When Coca-Cola was trying to really get started in Atlanta, several prominent Atlanta businessmen were offered the chance to invest in the new company. My grandfather declined, feeling that, as a lot of others did, the company wouldn't make it in the long run—a soft drink company, which had already been plagued with troubles, was not a wise investment. Oh boy! Did he regret that decision! And so, because it was a painful reminder when they had that soft drink in the house, Mana bought Canada Dry ginger ale instead! The ginger ale float was delicious anyway!

Put 2 scoops of vanilla ice cream in a tall glass and pour ginger ale over it—simple!

## ∾ **Mana's Tennessee Fruitcake** ∾

### *Truly a special recipe.*

1  pound each of raisins, currants, crystallized cherries, and dates
½  pound each of citron and candied lemon and orange peel, mixed
¾  pound sweet butter
3  cups packed dark brown sugar
8  eggs
⅔  cup molasses
1  teaspoon vanilla extract

2  teaspoons baking soda mixed into 3 tablespoons of water
½  cup bourbon or rum
4  cups flour
1  tablespoon cinnamon
1  teaspoon each of cloves, mace, allspice, and nutmeg
1  pound of either pecans or walnuts
Garnish — extra nut halves and candied cherries and citron

Prepare the fruits the day before, dusting with white sugar or extra flour. Have ingredients at room temperature. Cream butter and brown sugar. Add eggs, molasses, vanilla, baking soda mixed with water, and the whiskey. Sift together the flour and spices. Add flour/spice mixture a little at a time, beating constantly and making sure all is well incorporated. Lastly add the fruits and nuts. Mix very well. Put the batter in a well greased pan that is also lined with either waxed or parchment paper. Bake at 300 degrees for 2 hours. Thirty minutes before the cake is done, take the cake out of the oven and decorate the top with the extra nut halves and candied cherries. Return the cake to the oven and finish baking. Remove the cake from the oven and let it cool completely before removing from the pan. Remove the paper also. Place the cake in a cake tin with a whiskey-soaked cheesecloth draped over it. Put the top on the tin and place it in a cool dark place for 4 to 6 weeks to age. Every week remove the cheesecloth, re-wet it with the whiskey, re-drape the cake, and replace the closed tin in the cool place until the aging time is up. After cutting the cake, store in the tin with an apple that has been cut in half (this will keep the cake moist).

• *The fruits need to be well distributed throughout the cake. Of course, now you can buy them already cut and recipe ready. This is a very dense, dark fruitcake. You would probably like it even if you are not a fruitcake lover.*

• *You will need a deep round pan—a springform pan works well. This will make one cake. It can be doubled to make two.*

*When Mana made this fruitcake, she had to cut all of the dried fruits by hand, usually with scissors, and dust them with sugar so they wouldn't remain in globs.*

*There are as many variations of Brunswick Stew in Georgia as there are cooks who cook it! I loved Grandmother's and so did a lot of other folks in and around Bolton, Georgia. Bolton is a small community northwest of Atlanta. My grandmother and grandfather lived in a huge Victorian home that sat on a hill just outside Bolton. Every year, the church they belonged to, Collins Memorial Methodist Church, would have a "Homecoming On The Grounds" and every member and their children, grandchildren, brothers, sisters, aunts, uncles, cousins, and friends would come! Everybody brought a covered dish or a dessert.*

*Grandmother brought Brunswick Stew! People would stand in line for hours to get some of Mrs. McDonald's Brunswick Stew! It was and still is, in my estimation, the best! This recipe makes a large pot full. It can be doubled. I'm sure my grandmother had to make 10 times the recipe for Homecoming! It freezes beautifully. It is great with barbecue, fried chicken, or by itself.*

# Grandmother's
## ⌁ Famous Brunswick Stew ⌁

***This is a Southern dish that dates back to the earliest settlers of this country. They used squirrel, or possum, or whatever game they could find to put in the stew. I'm glad it has evolved to its current ingredients! Try it, you will like it…I Promise!!***

| | |
|---|---|
| 1 (5- to 6-pound) hen | ½ cup cider vinegar |
| 1 good-sized veal chop— 6 to 8 ounces | 1 teaspoon cayenne pepper |
| ½ pound calves liver | 2 tablespoons Lea & Perrins Worcestershire sauce |
| 1 large onion, diced | 2 tablespoons sugar |
| ¾ stick sweet butter | 1 tablespoon lemon juice |
| 2 (20-ounce) cans whole tomatoes, chop fine and reserve all juice | 2 (20-ounce) cans of creamed yellow corn |
| ½ cup ketchup | 1 small can tomato paste |
| | salt and pepper to taste |

In the stockpot, place the hen, the chop, and calves liver. Cover with water and cook over low heat until done. While the meat is cooking, sauté the onion in the butter until transparent. Set this aside. Remove the meat from the broth and save the broth. Chop the meat; return to the stockpot. Add the sautéed onion, and add enough of the reserved broth to cover by one inch. Add the next 7 ingredients. Cook over low heat for 2 hours, stirring often. After 2 hours, add the corn and tomato paste. Continue to cook over low heat for another hour. You will need to stir often to keep the corn from sticking to the bottom of the pan. Add salt and pepper to taste. Serves 12 to 16.

# Grandmother's
## ❧ Sweet Creamed Corn ❧

**enough ears of fresh white corn**
**to yield 2 cups of kernels —**
**6 or 8**
**2 tablespoons sweet butter**

**½ cup sugar**
**1 teaspoon salt**
**2 tablespoons flour**
**1½ cups milk**

Cut the corn off the cob and scrape the cob for the "milk." In a medium saucepan, melt the butter and add the corn, sugar, and salt. Cook over medium-low heat, stirring continually, until all of the sugar is dissolved — 3 to 5 minutes. Add the flour to the milk; blend with a fork until there are no lumps and stir into the corn. Continue stirring until everything is thick. Then, turn the heat to very low and cook for about 30 minutes, adding more milk (warmed first) if it seems to be too thick and stirring occasionally to be sure it doesn't stick to the bottom of the pan. Serves 6 to 8.

# Grandmother's
## ❧ Ambrosia ❧

Grandmother's Ambrosia was wonderful — fresh orange sections, sugar to taste, and fresh coconut. Simply super!

*I have made this with yellow corn, and it's good; but the flavor of yellow corn is somewhat different from white corn, so the dish has a different flavor. Try it both ways! It is better to make this when you can buy fresh corn. However, I have made it with Green Giant frozen Shoe Peg white corn and it is very close in taste to fresh.*

*These recipes are my interpretations of Grandmother's.*
*Unfortunately, it was too late to ask Grandmother for the originals.*
*They taste just like hers did.*

## ᘰ Rawls' Additions

• *I have added toasted pecans instead of almonds.*

• *I have added a small jar of diced pimentos.*

• *I have served this over biscuits and in puff pastry shells.*

# ᘰᴇ Grandmother's Turkey Hash ᴈᘰ

**We always went to Grandmother and Grandfather's big white
Victorian house on the hill at Christmas and Easter for brunch.
All of Daddy's brothers and sisters and their families were there too.
There were 26 in all!**

| | |
|---|---|
| 1 (10- to 12-pound) turkey | ½ cup of cornstarch |
| 6 ounces butter | salt and pepper to taste |
| 1 stalk of celery, diced finely | 1 cup of slivered almonds, |
| 1 large onion, diced finely |    toasted |
| 1 teaspoon sugar | |

Remove the giblets and the neck from the turkey. Cut the turkey into quarters and put in a large pot with the giblets and neck. Cover with water and bring to the boil. Turn the heat to low and simmer the turkey until done — 2 to 3 hours. Remove the turkey, giblets, and neck from the pot. Chop the turkey meat into bite-size pieces. Discard the neck and heart and chop the gizzard and liver into very small pieces. Reserve 1 cup of the broth. Return all of the meat to the remaining broth in the pot. In a fairly large skillet, melt the butter and sauté the diced celery and onion until transparent; then, add them to the pot. Add the sugar and simmer this over low heat for an hour. Dissolve the cornstarch in the reserved cup of broth and add this. Add salt and pepper. Cook until thickened. Just before serving, add the toasted almonds. Serve over Holland Rusk. Serves 6 to 12.

*At Christmas brunch we always had turkey hash on Holland Rusk,
baked ham, creamed corn, green beans, scalloped oysters, pickled
peaches, a relish tray, yeast rolls and biscuits, and ambrosia
served with fruitcake and pound cake for dessert.*

# Cooking Basics from Peggy

April 22, 1976

To Raleigh
With all my love every stitch
& hope I love you hope
you like it. I
love
Peggy

# *Peggy Cooks*
## *The "Basics" of Cooking from One of the Best Southern Cooks*

I probably wouldn't have collected any of the previous recipes if I had not developed
a love of cooking. But, I did and I still do love it. I was not taught the art of cooking at any
professional cooking school. I learned all of the basics, the techniques, how to make the
sauces, how to bake, all of the "how-tos" that I need to know to love Southern Cooking. . .
for that matter, all cooking, from a lady who was the best!

Peggy taught me how to cook. She almost never measured ingredients; she would
pour, scoop, put in a pinch of this or a dash of that. She taught me that if you knew
the basics by heart you wouldn't really ever need to measure.

I would come home from school, sit on the end stool at the counter in the kitchen
and watch her cook. We would talk and she would cook. Sometimes she would sing.
She had a glorious voice; she sounded a lot like a combination of Della Reese and
Mahalia Jackson. She even looked like a combination of Della Reese and Mahalia
Jackson! She was the choir president for many years at Ebenezer Baptist Church
in Atlanta. That's the church of Martin Luther King, Jr. and his family. Peggy and her
husband, Ozzie, knew all of the King family well. "Daddy" King, Dr. King, Sr., officiated
at her funeral in 1978. He had not been actively preaching for some time; but, he
honored her memory by officiating. I'm sure she was singing in heaven!

Peggy came to our family in 1950. I was six and, even then, would stay right under
Peggy's feet in the kitchen anxiously awaiting supper! Oh! The aromas! The first meal
she prepared for us was fried chicken, mashed potatoes and gravy, turnip greens, squash
casserole, baking powder biscuits, and chocolate pie for dessert! Boy, what a meal!

I loved watching Peggy cook. I loved talking to her, too. I guess I confided more secrets
and poured out more of my "teenager" woes to her than anyone else, even Momma.
Of course, I always knew that Peggy told Momma everything we talked about! It was just
easier, sometimes, to tell Peggy things. A lot of Moms want to jump right in before their
child has had a chance to finish saying anything; and as a result the child eventually
ceases trying to talk to his or her Mom. Because Peggy never ever criticized, she was the
one I talked to most of the time. By listening, she was actually helping me solve my own
problems. And. . .it was through listening to me that she showed me the importance of
listening—something I would carry through and later do with my own children! I learned
a lot sitting on that stool in the kitchen, watching and talking! A lot about a lot of things!

Peggy and Momma were soul mated—they were always there for each other. Peggy had the
"gift" too. . .she and Momma were almost eerie to be around sometimes. One time Momma
and Peggy did something awful. . .They put a "spell" on somebody—a hex! Thank goodness
after they thought about it, they had it removed before anything actually happened! Life with
them was very unusual to say the least! I never knew what was going to happen next!

Peggy and Momma both knew that Peggy would "leave" first—a fact that used to make Momma madder than a wet hen. When Peggy did "go" in 1978, Momma said that she was so mad at her that when she saw her in Heaven, she was going to "shoot" her!

I'm sure that they're up there now, making sure that I "write it down right"!

## Notes

*For a really special Dream Cream Sauce recipe, see page 46.*

## ⤺ Peggy's Dream Cream Sauce ⤻

*This makes a medium thick sauce.*

| | |
|---|---|
| 2 tablespoons butter | 2 tablespoons flour |
| 2½ cups milk | salt and white pepper to taste |

Melt the butter in the saucepan. Add 2 cups of the milk. Add the flour to the ½ cup of milk and stir with a fork until the mixture is smooth—no lumps. Add this to the hot milk in the saucepan, and stir until it is thick. The sauce needs to cook for at least 5 minutes to cook the flour. Add salt and white pepper to taste—use white pepper because it is not visible in the white sauce.

*Peggy taught me that a simple cream sauce can be the base of many other things.*

## Some Special Things ⤺ To Do With Cream Sauce ⤻

### Au Gratin Potatoes
Add 1½ cups of Cheddar cheese to make a cheese sauce. Pour this over sliced cooked potatoes in a casserole dish, adding more shredded cheese to the top.

### Macaroni and Cheese
Mix the cheese sauce with cooked macaroni. Put this in a casserole dish and sprinkle shredded cheese on top.

### Chicken Potpie
Add cubed chicken, cooked diced carrots, minced onion, green peas, and occasionally some pimento to the white sauce. Pour this in a casserole dish and top it with pastry crust.

# ~≪ Peggy's Fried Corn ≫~

### *A Very Southern Dish!*

Use "field" corn or white corn. You will need 2 ears for each person. Cut the kernels off the ears and scrape the ears for the "milk." Set aside. In a large skillet, fry 6 slices of bacon until done. Remove the bacon and set aside. Put the corn in the skillet with the bacon drippings and cook for 1 or 2 minutes, stirring well. Add 2 cups of water that you have mixed 2 tablespoons of flour into; add salt and pepper to taste, and stir until the corn is done. Crumble the bacon on top and serve.

# ~≪ How To Boil Corn ≫~

### *Never Tough!*

Remove the husks and silks from the corn and wash it. Place the corn in a large pot and fill with water. Add $1/4$ cup of sugar — no salt — to the water. Bring to the boil and cook for 1 minute. Turn the heat off, put a lid on the pot, and leave the lid on for 30 minutes. The corn will be done perfectly! Not adding salt is the secret — salt toughens the corn.

# ~≪ Ene's Fried Corn ≫~

"Ene" was Buck's grandmother and a sweetheart of a lady; and, although she didn't like to cook, she was a good cook. She fried her corn in bacon grease like Peggy did. She heated about $1/2$ cup bacon grease in a cast-iron skillet — this was for 12 ears of corn cut twice and scraped off the cob. She added the corn to the skillet with 2 tablespoons sugar and cooked this for 10 to 15 minutes, stirring constantly. Then, she added 3 cups of water and salt and pepper to taste. She cooked this, stirring often, over low heat for 1 hour. She occasionally would add more water to keep the corn from sticking.

## Notes

*Peggy always cooked a mixture of ¹/₂ turnip greens and ¹/₂ mustard greens. She cooked fresh string beans or pole beans this way too.*

## ᘓ Summer Squash ᘔ

### *Peggy always peeled squash before cooking it.*

| | |
|---|---|
| **10 large yellow squash, peeled and sliced** | **1 teaspoon sugar** |
| | **¹/₂ stick of butter** |
| **1 large onion, diced** | **salt and pepper to taste** |

Place the peeled and sliced squash in a large pot. Add the diced onion, sugar, and butter. Put water in the pot; it should only cover about ¹/₃ of the squash. Cook over low heat until the squash is tender. Add salt and pepper to taste. The reason you don't add much water is that the squash will release a lot of moisture as it cooks.

## ᘓ Squash Casserole ᘔ

Simply mash the cooked squash, add 2 beaten eggs, and put in a casserole dish. Place crushed saltine crackers on the top and dot with butter, making sure to use enough butter to evenly and completely cover the top. Place a sheet of aluminum foil over the top and place the casserole in a 350-degree oven. Bake for 40 minutes — remove the foil after 20 minutes to brown the top.

## ᘓ The Secret To Cooking "Greens" ᘔ

Very simply, the meat you cook with — ham, bacon, fatback, or streak o' lean — must be cooked first in the water you will cook the "greens" in — for at least 30 minutes! Peggy added 2 tablespoons of cider vinegar and 1 tablespoon of sugar to the water when she cooked the meat. That is the secret. Salt, pepper, and Tabasco sauce are added too, in amounts to suit personal tastes. Peggy always used small amounts of these. She said less was better — it is almost impossible to "save" a dish that is too salty or too hot. It's easier to start over.

## ᘓ Lima Beans Are Cooked Differently ᘔ

Cook lima beans until tender in water with a little salt in it. When they are tender, drain all but a small amount of the water, add butter and salt and pepper to taste and serve.

# ❧ Fried Green Tomatoes – Peggy's Way ❧

*Peggy used flour instead of cornmeal and*
*she fried them in bacon drippings.*

| | |
|---|---|
| 1 cup flour | 1 teaspoon salt |
| 1 teaspoon black pepper | 1 green tomato per person |
| shake of cayenne pepper | bacon drippings to fry them in |
| shake of white pepper | salt and black pepper to taste |
| 1 tablespoon of paprika | |

Combine 1 cup of flour with 1 teaspoon black pepper, a shake of cayenne pepper, a shake of white pepper, 1 tablespoon of paprika, and a teaspoon of salt. Mix this well. Cut the tomatoes into thin slices — 1/4 inch is about right. Press them in the seasoned flour, making sure they are well coated. You may need to flour each slice more than once. Heat the bacon drippings until very hot. Put the floured tomato slices in the hot drippings — be careful because the grease might splatter. Do not turn the slices over for about 3 minutes — if they are turned too soon they will lose their flour coating. You will only need to turn them once. After they are brown on both sides, remove from the grease and drain on brown paper (a grocery bag will do fine), or you can use paper towels. Sprinkle them with additional salt and black pepper if desired.

*Peggy also taught me the secret to making perfect rice.*

# ❧ Peggy's Perfect Rice ❧

For 4 servings: In a saucepan with a tightfitting lid, bring 3 cups of water to the boil. Add 1 1/2 cups rice (Peggy always used Uncle Ben's converted long grain rice), stir and immediately turn the heat down to the lowest setting, or to "warm," cover, and do not peek for 30 minutes. Then, turn the heat off, remove the cover, fluff the rice, and…Voila! Perfect Rice! Peggy did not add butter or salt to the water before cooking the rice. Butter, salt — and/or — pepper, should be added just before serving or by the person who's going to eat the rice. If you aren't going to be serving the rice for a while, transfer to a heatproof colander; and, like a double boiler, place the colander over a pot of water and cover. Before serving, bring the water in the pot to the boil to warm the rice. Works every time!

# ~ Wonderful Potatoes ~

### Baked Potatoes

For a baked potato with a crispy skin, rub the skin with solid Crisco and prick the skin a few times with a fork. Place the potatoes in a preheated 400-degree oven and bake until done. The time will vary according to the size of the potato—from 45 to 65 minutes. For a soft skin, do not rub with shortening, just prick the skin, wrap the potato in aluminum foil, and bake as described above.

### Stuffed Or Twice-Baked Potatoes

*For a puffy filling, add 2 eggs and beat well before stuffing the shells.*

For stuffed potatoes, bake the potato until done. Cut the potato in half and spoon the pulp into a small bowl. Add, for 4 potatoes, $1/2$ stick of butter, salt, pepper, and enough milk to make the potato slightly mushy—not runny. Mash with a fork, blending until rather smooth. Put the mixture back into the potato shells, sprinkle shredded Cheddar cheese on top (this is optional), and bake in a preheated 350-degree oven until the cheese has melted and the potato is hot.

### Mashed Potatoes

For mashed potatoes, Peggy peeled and sliced the potatoes, put the slices in a large pot, covered them with water, and cooked them until they were done. Then, she would drain them, put them through a potato ricer, add butter, milk, salt, and pepper and then beat them until fluffy—always by hand. For 6 potatoes she would add $1/2$ stick of butter and enough milk for them to be a creamy consistency—not runny. Her secret for fluffy potatoes was putting them through the ricer. I use an electric mixer.

### Candied Yams Or Sweet Potatoes

For 4 servings: Boil 5 or 6 yams/sweet potatoes in their skins until they are done. When done, peel them and slice or quarter them. Place them in a buttered rectangular or square baking pan. "Dot" evenly with a stick of butter. Mix together: 1 tablespoon cinnamon and 1 cup sugar; sprinkle over the potatoes. Bake at 350 degrees for 30 or 40 minutes or until syrupy.

*We always had these for Thanksgiving Eve Dinner and Christmas Eve Dinner. Since we always went to Grandmother's on Thanksgiving and Christmas, we had our family dinner the night before.*

### Marshmallow Sweet Potatoes

Boil 6 sweet potatoes with the skin left on. When done, peel and put through a ricer, or use a mixer. Add 1 stick of butter, $1/2$ cup packed brown sugar, $1/2$ cup white sugar, 1 tablespoon cinnamon, 1 teaspoon nutmeg, and 1 teaspoon allspice. Beat well, place in a buttered baking dish, put marshmallows on top, and bake at 350 degrees for 30 minutes.

# ~ Turkey 101 ~

I buy a frozen 20- to 22-pound "Old Tom."

Defrost the turkey in the refrigerator. Take the plastic wrapping off and remove the neck from the body cavity and the bag of giblets from under the flap of skin at the opposite end. Place the neck and giblets in a pan of water, and cook them until done, about 30 minutes. This will be the broth that you will use to make the stuffing.

Wash the turkey under running water. Let the water drain out and wipe the inside and outside of the turkey with paper towels to remove excess moisture. Prepare the roasting pan—Peggy used an old roaster that had a rack in the bottom and a top that was the same depth as the bottom. I line the bottom of the broiler pan that came with my oven with overlapping sheets of heavy duty-aluminum foil, making sure that there is enough foil to crimp all around, creating sides about 3 inches high. Then, I spray the foil well with Pam spray, and I place a roasting rack in the roasting pan to place the turkey on.

Rub the turkey well inside with 1 tablespoon of salt, and sprinkle some pepper inside also. Stuff the turkey with Peggy's Cornbread Stuffing (page 41), truss, and place in the roasting pan. Dot all over with 1 stick of butter. Put 2 cups of water in the bottom of the pan. Place the cover on the pan, put in a preheated 325-degree oven, and bake for 25 minutes a pound. I cover my turkey with a sheet of foil. You will need to baste the turkey a few times during the baking process and remove the cover/foil during the last hour of baking so that it will brown well.

The baking time of 25 minutes a pound is for a stuffed turkey. An unstuffed one should be baked for 20 minutes a pound at 325 degrees.

To prepare an unstuffed turkey, simply prepare it the same way as you prepare a stuffed one and omit the stuffing. Simple.

***The secrets to a golden brown, juicy turkey:***

*• Putting salt and pepper inside the turkey seasons the meat. If you put salt and pepper on the outside, you are only seasoning the skin. Butter the outside.*

*• The stuffing must be "wet" or mushy when you stuff a turkey—if you put a dry stuffing in the turkey, the stuffing will act like a sponge and draw moisture from the meat. A "wet" stuffing actually moistens the meat from the inside and the meat will be juicy.*

*• Putting the water in the pan when you begin baking—you are actually steaming the turkey, not roasting, until you uncover it to brown it. This keeps the meat moist. You leave it uncovered the last hour.*

*This recipe has never produced anything but a beautiful bird! I have never understood how anyone could be nervous about preparing a turkey. Think of a turkey as a big chicken!*

# ～ Notes

### Southern Fried Chicken

• *Fried chicken—the signature dish of the south. The dish that launched Kentucky Fried Chicken and served at every "meat and three" in the south. Of course, you all know that The Colonel didn't really fry his chicken—he had a secret cooking process, more like pressure cooking than frying. Anyway, The Colonel sure was a success with his way of "frying!"*

• *There are as many versions of the "right way" to fry chicken as there are Southerners in the South! I am giving you four versions— Peggy's, Grandmother's, Aunt Callie's, and Ene's. Of course, they are all different, and, yes, they all produce excellent fried chicken.*

## ～ Peggy's Fried Chicken ～

This recipe makes chicken that is crispy, crunchy, and tender…always! This recipe will fry 2 frying chickens—you may buy them already cut up or cut your own. First, wash the chicken by running the pieces under cold water. Then, combine 1/2 cup of salt and 4 cups of cold water; stir to dissolve the salt, and put the chicken pieces in this solution to soak for 30 minutes.

While the chicken is soaking, prepare an egg/milk "dip" by beating 2 eggs in 1 1/2 cups of cold milk in a bowl. In another—larger—bowl prepare the seasoned flour that you will flour the chicken with, by mixing: 1 teaspoon of cayenne pepper, 2 teaspoons of white pepper, 1 tablespoon of black pepper, 1/2 cup paprika, 1 teaspoon of salt, 2 teaspoons sugar, and 3 cups of flour. Mix this very well. Remove the chicken pieces from the salt water solution and pat dry with paper towels. Put 1 piece at a time in the egg/milk "dip," then into the seasoned flour. Roll each piece well in the flour, place on a platter—side by side, not piled on top of each other. You will flour the chicken a second time—just before putting the pieces in the skillet to fry.

Choose a large skillet—cast-iron, if you prefer—it should be a rather heavy one. Put the skillet over high heat and put 3 cups of Crisco solid shortening in the skillet to heat. It will take a few minutes to get the shortening hot enough to fry the chicken, so use this time to flour the pieces you will cook first. The dark meat takes longest to cook. Test if the Crisco is hot by putting a piece of the chicken in the pan. It will "sizzle" and really begin to "fry" if it is hot enough. If it doesn't, just leave the piece in the pan until it does! Then you can add more pieces—do not crowd the chicken in the pan.

Do not turn the chicken until you are sure the side that is currently in the shortening has browned slightly. Don't turn the pieces too many times—2 is enough. The chicken is done when the juices run clear when the piece is pricked with a fork. Keep the heat medium-high so that the crust doesn't brown too much before the meat is done. Continue reflouring and cooking until all pieces are done. Drain the pieces on paper towels or brown grocery bags. The second flouring makes a crispy crust and keeping the oil evenly hot, insures it.

***Very, very, important…*** If you plan to cook the liver, you must pierce many times with a fork before dipping in the egg/milk dip and flouring and frying. Why? Because this keeps the liver from "popping" and splattering grease all over everything—especially you! Hot grease burns and makes a yucky mess! The secret—soaking in salt water. Peggy said it "drew out" excess blood, something I'm sure started way back, when you killed your own. Nevertheless, it was what she did and I do, too.

## ～ Grandmother's Different Fried Chicken ～

To begin with, she raised the chickens. So, when she was planning to fry chicken for supper, she had one killed. It was much later that she would buy chicken from the market. She always soaked her chicken in fresh buttermilk before she floured it. She fried her chicken in bacon drippings, or a combination of Crisco and bacon drippings. This makes for a dark brown crust and a softer crust because you have to keep the grease at a lower temperature to prevent the grease from "smoking" if you use bacon drippings. Her fried chicken had a wonderful flavor.

# ~~ Fried Chicken Gravy ~~

### Serve over Peggy's Mashed Potatoes, Perfect Rice, or…yum, yum…Baking Powder Biscuits!!

Pour all but about $1/2$ cup shortening from the pan. There will be quite a lot of "crumbs" in the pan also; don't remove this from the pan, it "makes" the gravy. Add $1/2$ cup of the seasoned flour that's left over from flouring the chicken. Stir this for 2 or 3 minutes over medium-high heat—this will cook the flour and the gravy won't taste pasty. Add 2 cups of hot water and stir vigorously, until the gravy thickens. You may need more hot water—use your own judgment—gravy thickness is a personal thing. What's thick to some may be thin to others!

* For Mashed Potatoes, see page 34.

* For Perfect Rice, see page 33.

* For Old-Fashioned Baking Powder Biscuits, see page 40.

# ~~ Aunt Callie's Fried Chicken ~~

I use this recipe a lot when I fry boneless breast pieces. Put the breasts in a large bowl and cover with a mixture of 1 tablespoon Tabasco sauce and $1/2$ gallon buttermilk. Depending on the number of chicken breasts you have, this may have to be doubled because the chicken must be completely covered. Place the bowl in the refrigerator and leave overnight or at least 8 hours. Pour in a colander to drain. Flour one piece at a time in a mixture of $1 1/2$ cups flour seasoned with 2 teaspoons pepper and 1 teaspoon salt. Fry in hot shortening or oil, turning once, until done and crispy brown. This makes chicken with a really crusty crust.

* Aunt Callie is Callie Patton McDonald.

* She was married to my father's oldest brother, Harold. She and Uncle Harold had two sons, Harold, Jr., and Larry. Larry was a U.S. Congressman from Georgia. If you ever drive into Atlanta on I-75, you can't miss the big sign on the right just after you cross the Cobb County — Fulton County line that says "Larry P. McDonald Memorial Highway." Yep, that's her son and my cousin! Anyway, Aunt Callie is a great cook. She taught Home Economics and Cooking classes in Fulton County High School. I was a guest in one of her classes when I was 8 years old. She is a special lady and I have included some of the recipes she has given me over the past 45 years.

# ~~ Ene's Fried Chicken ~~

Buck's grandmother did her chicken a bit differently, too. She rinsed the chicken pieces and patted them dry. Then, she mixed $1 1/2$ cups of flour, 1 teaspoon salt, 1 teaspoon paprika, and $1/8$ teaspoon pepper in a paper bag. She dipped each piece of the chicken in $1 1/2$ cups of milk; then, put it in the bag, shook the bag to flour it well, and placed the piece in hot oil. She let the chicken cook on one side, until that side was golden brown. She turned the chicken and lowered the heat slightly, cooking for about 5 minutes. Then, she covered the pan, and let the chicken cook, covered, for about 10 minutes. Then, she uncovered the pan and turned the heat back up to brown and crisp the chicken, turning once more. She made her gravy with milk, pouring most of the grease from the pan, adding 3 tablespoons flour and scraping the browned bits in the skillet as the flour cooked. When the flour was browned, she added milk to get the consistency she wanted, added salt and pepper to taste, and served the gravy with the chicken.

# ✑ Notes

### The secrets

• *Rubbing the lamb with vinegar.*

• *Baking at 400 degrees at first.*

## ⟶ Peggy's Leg Of Lamb ⟵

Momma would buy a whole leg—5 pounds, or so, and have the butcher remove the hard piece of cartilage under the skin near the hip joint that Peggy called "the deaf ear." She said this would remove "the gamey taste." This is not a necessary step today. Begin by trimming some of the excess fat from the lamb. Leave some. Rub the whole leg with cider vinegar, sprinkle well with salt and pepper, and place in a roasting pan that has a lid. (Wrapping with heavy-duty foil will work also.) Place in a preheated 400-degree oven. Cover and bake at this temperature for 15 minutes, then, lower the temperature to 350 degrees. At this point, completely coat the lamb with this sauce:

**2 cups of ketchup**　　　　　　**1 large onion, diced**
**1 cup French's yellow mustard**

Continue to bake, covered, for 2 hours. After 1 hour, spoon the remaining sauce over the lamb. Cover again and bake for 30 minutes. Remove the cover and finish baking. The lamb will be tender on the inside and crusty on the outside.

Peggy made the gravy this way: Remove the lamb from pan and pour the grease from the pan. Combine $1/2$ cup of flour with 1 cup of water. Stir well with a fork—there should be no lumps—and deglaze the pan. Stir constantly and add water as needed to achieve a thick smooth gravy.

*The lamb everybody loved—the only one my children would eat and one of my favorite comfort foods!*

## ⟶ Peggy's Special Hamburgers ⟵
### *What memories these bring back!*

First, patty the burgers, using ground round. Heat a large skillet. When the pan is hot, layer each burger in this order:

**1 tablespoon A.1. sauce**　　　**a shake of Lea & Perrins**
**1 tablespoon Heinz 57 sauce**　**Worcestershire sauce**
**1 ounce butter**

Place the patty on top, sprinkle each patty with Lawry's seasoned salt, pepper, and just a dab of A.1. and 57 sauce on top of the burger. After 2 or 3 minutes, flip the burgers, press them very lightly with a spatula, and sprinkle with the seasoned salt and pepper. Continue to flip and press the burgers until they are done to your liking. They are the best!!

# ⤜ Peggy's Stuffed Red Snapper ⤛

### *The whole fish, an elegant recipe.*

4  slices stale bread
10 or 12 saltine crackers,
   crumbled
1  small onion, diced
4  ribs celery, diced
¼ cup butter
2  tablespoons minced parsley
salt and pepper
½ teaspoon cayenne pepper

1  teaspoon Lea & Perrin's
   Worcestershire sauce
1  large whole red snapper,
   3 to 4 pounds dressed, with
   the head on
4  bacon slices
1  stick butter
juice of 1 lemon

First, make the bread stuffing: Place bread that you have torn into small pieces into a bowl. Add crumbled crackers. Pour hot water over to make it wet. Set aside. In a skillet, sauté onion and celery in butter. When limp, add to the bread. Add parsley and salt and pepper. Add cayenne pepper and Worcestershire sauce; mix well.

Rinse the fish in cold running water. Pat dry. Stuff the fish with the stuffing. Tie a piece of twine or string around the fish to hold the stuffing inside. Place the fish on a rack in a well greased baking pan. Lay the 4 pieces of bacon across the fish and place in a preheated 350-degree oven. Bake for 30 to 40 minutes or until browned. Remove the fish from the oven and let it sit for a few minutes. Cut the twine and serve the fish with the stuffing.

Make a brown butter-lemon sauce by heating 1 stick of butter in a skillet, watching closely, until it is a nutty brown color. Add the juice of 1 lemon; stir quickly. Serve over the fish.

## Rawls' ⤜ Additions

*I have cooked this recipe with a crab meat stuffing that is made by reducing the amount of bread to 2 slices and omitting the saltines. Mix in 8 ounces of backfin crab meat (that you have picked over to remove any bits of shell or cartilage) with a fork. Mix and mash it well, then stuff it into the fish and proceed with the recipe. It is really special.*

*For the secret recipes for biscuits from one famous Nashville cafe and a restaurant chain, see pages 64 and 65.*

# Old-Fashioned
## ~ Baking Powder Biscuits ~

*Light and fluffy! This recipe makes 8 to 10 biscuits, depending on the size they are cut.*

| | | | |
|---|---|---|---|
| 2 | cups flour | ½ | teaspoon salt |
| 1 | tablespoon double-acting baking powder | ½ | cup solid Crisco |
| | | ½ to ⅔ | cup very cold milk |

Sift together the flour, baking powder, and salt into a large mixing bowl. Cut in the shortening with a pastry blender or two knives. Add the cold milk, stirring with a fork until the dough forms a moist ball. This should take about ½ to ⅔ cup. Roll out on a floured surface to ½ inch thick. Be careful not to overwork the dough — it makes tough biscuits! Cut with a floured biscuit cutter or glass. Place on a greased baking sheet. Bake in a 400-degree oven until browned — about 10 to 12 minutes.

### For "Drop" Biscuits
Increase the cold milk to 1¼ cups, and "drop" on the baking sheet.

*Peggy would stay with me and my brothers — Johnny and Morris — when Momma and Daddy would go out of town and she always made these wonderful waffles.*

## ~ Sunday Night Waffles ~

*This batter will keep for up to two weeks in the refrigerator — we never had any left to leave in the refrigerator!*

| | | | |
|---|---|---|---|
| 2 | cups flour | 2 | tablespoons sugar |
| 1 | tablespoon double-acting baking powder | 1½ | cups sweet milk |
| ½ | teaspoon salt | 3 | eggs |
| | | 1 | stick butter, melted |

Sift the flour, baking powder, and salt into a large mixing bowl. Add the sugar and the milk. Add the eggs and beat well. Add the melted butter, beating well to incorporate. Refrigerate the batter for at least 1 hour before using. Serve the waffles with melted butter, syrup, or honey poured on top. Yummmm...!

### Pancakes

*Peggy used this same batter — adding more milk to thin it — for pancakes. Sometimes, she used buttermilk instead of the sweet milk. She added a teaspoon of vanilla extract sometimes, also. The vanilla was a nice touch.*

# ~≈ Southern Cornbread ≈~

### *This is true Southern Cornbread —*
### *old-fashioned southern cornbread was not sweet!*

¾ cup solid Crisco
2 cups of cornmeal
½ cup flour
½ teaspoon salt
1 teaspoon baking soda

1 tablespoon double-acting baking powder
2 eggs
1 to 1½ cups milk or buttermilk — enough to make a creamy batter

FIRST, you must preheat the oven to 400 degrees. Before mixing the batter, put ¾ cup solid Crisco into the 9-inch metal pan (glass will break) and put the pan in the preheated 400-degree oven. Then, in a large mixing bowl, combine the dry ingredients; stir well. Stir in the eggs. Add the milk—start with 1 cup. Add the ½ cup gradually until you have a creamy, not runny, batter.

Now for the tricky part: being very careful, take the pan with the melted shortening out of the oven and pour the hot shortening over the batter. Working quickly and carefully, stir the hot shortening into the batter, making sure it is completely incorporated. Pour the batter back into the pan and put the pan back in the oven to bake for 30 to 35 minutes or until browned.

• *Try substituting bacon drippings for the Crisco—just don't heat for very long in the oven, it will really smoke!!*

• *For Aunt Callie's Sour Cream Cornbread recipe, see page 108. It is a really good one; albeit, it is more like a "Southern spoonbread."*

# ~≈ Peggy's Cornbread Stuffing ≈~

### *A very old recipe! This will make enough stuffing*
### *for a 20-pound turkey, and bake an extra pan full, too.*

½ loaf of white bread, left out overnight to "stale"
1 recipe Southern Cornbread
1 sleeve Nabisco saltine crackers

1 stalk of celery, diced
2 onions, diced
salt, pepper, and poultry seasoning to taste

First, make the broth: Remove the giblets and the neck from the turkey. Place them in a large pot, cover with water, and cook until done, about 30 minutes.

Tear the stale bread into very small pieces and place in a large mixing bowl. Crumble the cornbread and the saltines. Add this along with the celery and onions to the bowl; mix well. Add the broth a cup at a time until the stuffing is mushy—it should be wet! Add salt, pepper, and poultry seasoning to taste.

Stuff the bird or put in a large baking dish and bake at 350 degrees for 40 to 50 minutes or until done. If a shallow pan is used, the cooking time will be shorter.

• *For how to cook the turkey, see page 35.*

• *Instead of using the stale bread and the saltines, I use Pepperidge Farm Herb Seasoned Stuffing. It is one of those shortcut products that I use that doesn't change the flavor of the dish and it makes the preparation easier. I use one small bag and mix it with the onion, celery, homemade cornbread, the giblet broth, and the seasonings. Simple!*

# A Georgia Chocolate Cake— ~ From Scratch! ~

*This makes a scrumptious 2-layer cake or 1-layer sheet cake!!!*

## For the cake:

| | |
|---|---|
| 1½ cups flour | ⅔ cup Crisco oil |
| 1¼ teaspoons baking soda | 1 cup buttermilk |
| 1 teaspoon double-acting baking powder | 1 teaspoon vanilla extract |
| 1 teaspoon salt | 2 eggs |
| ½ cup Hershey's cocoa | 1¼ cups sugar |

## For the frosting:

| | |
|---|---|
| 8 ounces Philadelphia cream cheese, at room temperature | 1 box 10x confectioners' sugar |
| 1 tablespoon milk | 1 teaspoon vanilla extract |
| 3 squares unsweetened chocolate, melted and cooled | ¼ teaspoon salt |

Sift the first 5 ingredients into a large mixing bowl. Add the oil, buttermilk, and vanilla; beat well. Beat the eggs and sugar together until the mixture is fluffy. Add this to the batter and beat well. Pour the batter into 2 well greased and waxed paper-lined cake pans or a sheet cake pan. Bake in a preheated 350-degree oven for 25 to 30 minutes or until done. Remove from the pan(s), let cool and frost the cake.

Beat the room temperature cream cheese with the milk. Add the melted and cooled chocolate; mix well. Add the box of confectioners' sugar, the vanilla, and the salt. Beat until fluffy.

# ❧ Peggy's Fabulous Fudge Cake ❧

### *Wonderful with a scoop of ice cream on top!!*

| | |
|---|---|
| 1 stick butter, at room temperature | 2 eggs |
| 1 cup sugar | ½ cup flour |
| 2 squares unsweetened chocolate, melted and cooled | ¼ teaspoon salt |
| 1 teaspoon vanilla extract | ½ cup chopped walnuts, pecans, or almonds |

Cream together the butter and sugar. Add the melted chocolate and vanilla; beat well. Beat in the eggs. Add the flour, salt, and the nuts; mix well. Pour into a well greased cake pan and bake in a preheated 325-degree oven for 30 to 35 minutes.

# ❧ Old Southern Pound Cake ❧

### *A delicious cake. Truly a "pound" cake.*

| | |
|---|---|
| 1 pound butter, at room temperature | 12 eggs |
| 1 pound box 10x confectioners' sugar | 1 pound flour (after emptying the confectioners' sugar, fill the box with flour) |
| 1 tablespoon vanilla extract | |

In a large mixing bowl, cream the butter with the confectioners' sugar until fluffy. Add the vanilla. Add the eggs 1 at a time, beating well after each addition. Fill the empty confectioners' sugar box to the top with flour. Sift the flour and add it a little at a time, beating well, until all the flour is incorporated. Put the batter into an angel food cake pan and bake in a preheated 325-degree oven for 1 to 1½ hours. Begin testing for doneness after 1 hour by inserting a "broom straw" into the cake. If it comes out "clean," the cake is done.

# Peggy's Orange Juice Coffee Cake

*Not too sweet, just right.*

**For the cake:**

| | |
|---|---|
| 1 cup flour | 1 egg |
| ½ cup sugar | ½ stick butter, melted |
| 2 teaspoons double-acting baking powder | ¼ cup orange juice |
| | ¼ cup milk |
| ½ teaspoon salt | 1 teaspoon vanilla extract |

**For the crumb topping:**

| | |
|---|---|
| 3 tablespoons sugar | 1 teaspoon cinnamon |
| 1 tablespoon flour | 3 tablespoons butter |

Sift into a mixing bowl the flour, sugar, baking powder, and salt. Add the egg, melted butter, orange juice, milk, and vanilla. Beat very well. Pour into a well greased 9-inch square pan and bake in a preheated 325-degree oven for a total of 25 to 30 minutes. The crumb topping should be sprinkled on top of the cake after it has been in the oven for 20 minutes.

To make the crumb topping: Blend together the topping ingredients with a fork until well blended and crumbly. Simple!

# Marshmallow Frosting
## For Cakes_Any Cake!

| | |
|---|---|
| 1½ cups sugar | 6 large marshmallows |
| ½ cup water | 1 teaspoon vanilla extract |
| 2 egg whites | |

Cook the sugar and water until it comes to the soft-ball stage. Beat the egg whites until stiff. When the sugar syrup is ready, remove from the heat and add the 6 marshmallows and the vanilla. Gently "swirl" the syrup to incorporate the marshmallows and vanilla. Slowly pour the hot syrup over the egg whites, beating with the beater set on high speed the whole time. Continue to beat on high until the frosting is smooth and fluffy. Frost the cake immediately.

# Peggy's Pies

## ≈ Pastry For Any Pie ≈

Sift 2 cups flour and $1/2$ teaspoon salt into a mixing bowl. "Cut" into this $3/4$ cup solid Crisco with a pastry blender or two knives. Add just enough ice water to make a ball of pastry—start with $1/4$ cup. The ball should just hold together and not be too "wet." Divide in half and roll out, fairly thin, on a floured surface.

*Chilled butter may be substituted for all or part of the Crisco.*

## ≈ Apple Pie ≈

### *This recipe makes one pie. The absolute best apple pie!!*

*I have added $1/2$ cup of dark raisins—Delicious.*

**Pie pastry**
**8 Granny Smith apples, peeled, cored, and sliced**
**the juice of $1/2$ lemon**
**2 teaspoons vanilla extract**
**$1\frac{1}{2}$ cups sugar**
**$1/4$ cup flour**
**$1/2$ teaspoon salt**
**1 teaspoon each cinnamon and allspice**
**$1/2$ teaspoon nutmeg**
**1 stick butter**

Prepare the pie pastry. Place the sliced apples in a large mixing bowl, toss with the lemon juice and the vanilla. Sprinkle the sugar, flour, salt and spices over the apples; toss extremely well. Put in a pastry-lined pie plate; dot the butter evenly on top of the apples. Place pastry on top, trim any excess, flute the edges, and cut several slits in the top. Make a hole in the center of the top pastry for steam to escape. Place in a cold oven. Turn the oven temperature to 375 degrees and bake for 45 to 50 minutes or until well browned.

## ✺ Notes

*Peggy said this was the way it got its name: Many years ago it was a tradition in the South to take a cake, pie, or casserole to someone's home if they were sick, or to the "wake" after a death. One lady, not having anything to make a pie out of but some eggs, some sugar, and some butter, decided to use exactly those things. She made her pie and took it. When asked what kind of pie she had made, the lady replied, "It's jes pie." And so, over the years the name became "chess"!*

## ✺ Southern Chess Pie ✺

***I have added a bag of semisweet chocolate chips. When baked, the chips rise to the top! This chocolate pie is my family's all-time favorite!***

| | |
|---|---|
| **3 eggs** | **2 teaspoons vanilla extract** |
| **1½ cups sugar** | **1 tablespoon cider vinegar** |
| **1 stick butter, melted** | **1 tablespoon cornmeal** |
| **¼ teaspoon salt** | **1 unbaked pie shell** |

Place all of the ingredients except the pie shell in a mixing bowl and beat well. Pour into the unbaked pie shell and put in a preheated 325-degree oven. Bake for 60 to 70 minutes. Remove from the oven and let it cool completely before cutting. I have added a small can of coconut and it is delicious.

## ✺ Georgia Pecan Pie ✺

| | |
|---|---|
| **3 eggs** | **6 tablespoons butter, melted** |
| **⅔ cup packed brown sugar** | **¼ teaspoon salt** |
| **½ cup dark Karo corn syrup** | **1½ cups whole pecans** |
| **2 teaspoons vanilla extract** | **1 unbaked pie shell** |

Put the eggs into a mixing bowl. Beat them with the brown sugar, Karo, vanilla, butter, and the salt. Add the pecans; stir well. Pour in the unbaked pie shell. Place in a preheated 425-degree oven and bake for 6 minutes. Turn the heat down to 325 degrees and bake for 30 to 35 minutes. Remove from the oven and cool completely before cutting. Sinfully good!

## ✺ Chocolate Cream Pie ✺

*For Peggy's Dream Cream Sauce, see page 30.*

Peggy would prepare a recipe of her cream sauce but she would omit the pepper and add 3 egg yolks, 3 squares of melted unsweetened chocolate, 1 cup of sugar, 2 teaspoons vanilla extract, ¼ teaspoon cinnamon and put into a prebaked pie shell. She would top the pie with Meringue, and put the pie in a 350-degree oven to brown the Meringue. She just made her Famous Chocolate Cream Pie!

### Meringue
She made the Meringue by adding ½ teaspoon cream of tartar to the 3 egg whites — while beating along with ½ cup sugar and continuing to beat until stiff peaks form.

# Rawls and Friends

# Rawls and Friends

Buck and I love to entertain. We have a large seated dinner party for 12 or 14 each
Christmas. We have small casual dinners every 4 to 6 weeks. But, my favorite kind of party
is a cocktail supper. Why? Because, I always do all of the cooking and just about everything
can be prepared ahead of time, arranged on serving platters and refrigerated, or heated
beforehand and kept warm. I have fun creating new and different dishes and I always
include a dish that is not usually presented as an hors d'oeuvre.

As I plan the menu, I create — I only use my cookbooks for ideas. Basically, I am able to
create new recipes as I plan. I start with a "basic" and add whatever sounds good to my
taste buds at the moment. Even though I jot down a few notes on what the new idea is,
it usually gets changed a little when I prepare.

When someone asks how I did that, I'm not kidding when I reply that "I didn't really
have a recipe." I'm sure that some thought I just didn't share my recipes — well, this
cookbook should set that straight!

I'm telling all I remember and all I know about how I cook! Since I rarely — almost never —
write any of my creations down, I will be remembering mostly. And creating more as I go.

I have a remarkable memory — thank the Lord!

## Rawls' Additions

• *I love to use other cheeses — like Camembert, Havarti, Gouda, Farmer's cheese, and Monterey Jack. They all do as well as the Brie.*

• *Some fun ways to do Baked Monterey Jack:*

• *Put seasoned refried beans and/or chopped green chiles on top,*

• *Top with chopped onion, tomato, jalapeño, and corn,*

• *Put avocado slices, onion slices, and sun-dried tomato pieces on top.*

*This is a McCall's/Sonoma Sun-Dried Tomato Pesto Contest Prize Winner.*

# ~ Different Brie ~

### *I always wrap the cheese in Pepperidge Farm puff pastry sheets that have been rolled thin.*

### Sweet Brie-in-a-Bag

After placing the cheese on the pastry, put a mound of dark brown sugar on top of the cheese. Press down to compress the sugar and put either almonds, pecans, or walnuts on top of the sugar. Wrap the pastry around the cheese, making sure the entire thing is completely encased. Twist at the top to resemble a twisted bag. Brush with an egg wash (beat an egg well and brush it on) if desired. Place on an ungreased baking sheet and bake in a preheated 400-degree oven until well browned.

### Zesty Brie-in-a-Bag

Instead of the sugar and nuts, spread the pastry with Dijon mustard, place the cheese on top, and put a mound of shaved ham on top of the cheese. Sprinkle with poppy seeds or Durkees canned fried onions, encase with the pastry, and bake as above.

# ~ Pastry Presto ~

**Process:**

  2  cups tightly packed basil leaves
  1/2 cup extra-virgin olive oil
  2  cloves of garlic, sliced
  1/4 cup pine nuts

**Mix and Set Aside:**

  1/2 cup freshly grated Parmesan cheese
  1/4 cup freshly grated Romano cheese
  1/2 cup coarsely chopped dried tomatoes (not marinated)

**Puff Pastry:**

  1  sheet puff pastry, at room temperature
 12 fresh spinach leaves
  1 1/2 red onions, thinly sliced
 12 ounces fontina cheese, cubed

  1/2 cup sliced black olives
  1  teaspoon crushed red pepper flakes
Freshly ground pepper to taste

Brush the puff pastry lightly with olive oil. Place 6 of the spinach leaves in the center of the pastry in a circle approximately 6 inches in diameter. Place the thinly sliced onions on top of the spinach leaves. Place the cubed fontina cheese on top of the onions (remaining in the circle). Sprinkle the olives on the cheese. Add the red pepper flakes and a few grinds of fresh pepper. Spoon 3 tablespoons of the dried tomato pesto over this. Lay the remaining spinach leaves on top and enclose this in the pastry by gathering the 4 corners up and twisting the top to resemble a paper bag. Place on an ungreased baking sheet. Place in a preheated 400-degree oven and bake until the pastry is golden brown — 20 to 30 minutes. Let cool to warm before cutting into wedges. Enjoy!!! Serves 10 to 12.

# Fun Things To Do
## With A Pizza Or Focaccia Shell

### Brie Boboli

I created this for a Steeplechase Party a few years ago. I brushed a Boboli crust with olive oil (I use extra-virgin Bertolli), overlapped fresh spinach leaves on top, cut up a small wheel of Brie, and put this on top of the spinach. I placed this on a pizza pan and put it in a preheated 400-degree oven and baked until the cheese melted. It got raves! I gave this recipe to a friend, Anne Byrn Whitaker, food writer for Nashville's morning newspaper, *The Tennessean*. She included the recipe in an article in *The Tennessean* this past December, so this one isn't exactly a secret—but it is too easy and too good to leave out!

### Basil-Oregano-Feta Boboli

Again, brush the crust with oil, and this time, overlap fresh basil leaves on top and sprinkle with fresh oregano and lots of feta cheese. Bake as described above. Wonderful!

*Be inventive and try some ideas of your own on ready-made crusts.*

### Pesto-Prosciutto-Romano Boboli

And another: Spoon basil pesto on the crust, and sprinkle with chopped prosciutto. Put a little shredded Romano on and bake as above.

### Boboli Wedges

I love to use Boboli as the bread when I serve lasagna or any pasta. I simply brush the Boboli with a lot of My Garlic Oil, sprinkle with a small amount of shredded Parmesan cheese, bake until well browned, cut into wedges, and serve. It is a hit—always!

## My Garlic Oil

I keep a bottle of homemade garlic olive oil in my kitchen all the time. To make it, simply put 2 or 3 cut up garlic cloves in the bottom of a bottle and pour extra-virgin olive oil in the bottle. It keeps a good while. If the garlic gets real dark, you will need to discard the garlic and, possibly, the oil—if it smells old and rancid. I use it all the time, adding more oil as needed and adding fresh garlic, so I don't have the problem of old oil.

# Notes

*I love to roll things in burrito-sized flour tortillas, and in bread dough. I am not fond of using moistened flatbread—it takes longer to prepare and is more trouble than using a flour tortilla. I also do not use filo dough much; I like the results but not the hassle. I do have two or three brunch recipes that I am including that call for filo that are fairly easy.*

## Your Turn!

*Pick a type of cuisine you like, think of what seasonings are used in cooking it and what fruits, vegetables, or meats are used in it. Lay the foods in strips, or evenly and thinly sprinkled, and roll.*

# Rollers

### Scottish Smoked Salmon Rollers

Scottish smoked salmon is traditionally served with cream cheese (or butter) and chopped onion and capers. I love capers, but the little things are really hard to keep on the salmon when you try to take a bite! So, quite a few years ago, I hit upon the idea of mixing the cream cheese, onion, and capers together and putting the mixture in a serving bowl surrounded by the sliced salmon and toast. This was a very easy way to serve it and I have been doing this ever since.

This past Christmas, I realized that I didn't have enough Scottish smoked salmon to do a whole platter, so I decided to "roll" it. I spread the cream cheese mix on the tortilla, placed the salmon slices on top, rolled it up, and when it was well chilled, I sliced the rolls in 1-inch slices. Everybody loved them.

### Cream Cheese-Onion-Caper Spread

Simply mix 16 ounces Neufchâtel cheese (it's softer than cream cheese) with $1/2$ medium onion, finely diced, and a small jar of drained capers. I have also added a touch ($1/2$ teaspoon) of dillweed on occasion.

# Other Things To Roll

**Pimento Cheese Rolls**—Spread Rawls' Pimento Cheese (page 21) on tortilla and sprinkle with chopped parsley and roll.

**Mexican Rolls**—Mix 8 ounces softened Neufchâtel cheese with 1 tablespoon of dried cilantro, 1 teaspoon ground cumin, 2 teaspoons chili powder (I use Spice Islands Chili Con Carne Seasoning), and a can of chopped green chiles. Spread on tortillas. Add thinly sliced strips of green pepper, whole green onions, seeded chopped tomato, and sliced jalapeños and roll.

**Spinach-Asparagus-Mushroom Rolls**—Mix 8 ounces softened Neufchâtel cheese, 2 cloves minced garlic, 1 teaspoon coarse grind black pepper, and $1/4$ teaspoon grated nutmeg. Spread on tortillas, add spinach leaves, asparagus spears, and thinly sliced mushrooms in rows and roll.

**Basil-Artichoke Rolls**—Spread the cheese mixture on tortillas, add basil leaves, artichoke heart pieces, black olive slices, bits of sun-dried tomato, and toasted pine nuts in rows and roll.

**Roast Beef-Horseradish-Bacon Rolls**—Mix a roll of Kraft garlic cheese with 3 ounces cream cheese and 1 tablespoon prepared horseradish. Spread on tortillas, lay roast beef slices and crisp bacon strips on top, and roll.

# ~◎ Bread Rolls ◎~

I use Pillsbury French bread dough or Pillsbury pizza dough — find them in tubes in the dairy. After unrolling the tube and taking the dough out, unroll the dough and place on a well greased sheet of heavy-duty aluminum foil and place it in a jelly roll pan. Refrigerate. Keep it cold until you are ready to put the ingredients on it because it will stretch too much when you roll it.

### Fun Things to Roll in Bread Dough

Always brush the dough with oil before putting the ingredients on. I use My Garlic Oil (page 53).

### Italian Meats and Cheese-Stuffed Bread

I have used an assortment of meats — prosciutto, Italian salami, sliced pepperoni — and mixed them as I placed them on the dough. Then sprinkle with a bit of shredded mozzarella. Roll the dough, pinch the seams to seal, and bake in a preheated 375-degree oven for 30 minutes or until well browned. Let cool for 10 or 15 minutes before slicing.

### Italian Sausage-Onion-Green Pepper Bread

Use thin slices of onion and green pepper and cooked, crumbled Italian sausage — be sure to rinse the sausage under hot water to remove the grease after cooking. Add shredded mozzarella and roll and bake as above.

*I think the possibilities are endless –*
*use your imagination and what you like. Have Fun!*

### Ham-Sauerkraut Bread

Oh! So good is shaved ham, drained and rinsed shredded sauerkraut, sliced sweet gherkins, and Swiss cheese slices. Roll and bake as above.

### Four-Cheese Bread

I like sharp white Cheddar, Swiss, shredded Parmesan, and crumbled feta. Sprinkle with cracked black pepper and roll and bake as above.

### Caramelized Onion-Mushroom-Spinach Bread

Sautéed mushrooms, spinach (chopped, cooked, and drained), shredded Monterey Jack cheese, and caramelized onions (place 2 thinly sliced onions in a skillet with a tablespoon of butter and cook over medium heat, stirring very often to prevent burning, until they are a deep golden color). Roll up and bake as above.

**Notes**

## ᕠ Some Other Salmon Recipes ᕠ

When I serve Northwest smoked salmon — the kind from Harry and David or Norm Thompson — I serve it with a sweet-tart Mustard Dill Sauce. I first made this to try and duplicate a sauce Buck described to me that he had had in Iceland. When he was President and CEO of Winners Corporation, he went on a salmon fishing trip with some Pepsi-Cola executives. He had salmon prepared as Gravlax, a dill- and salt-cured salmon, and it was served with a mustard dill sauce. I was able to create a sauce that pretty much duplicated it. An Englishman, whose wife was from Iceland, attended one of our parties. I served this sauce with some Scottish Salmon, and he commented that he thought it "one of the best he had tasted." That made me feel pretty good.

### Mustard Dill Sauce

Put $3/4$ cup of sugar in a saucepan, add $1/2$ cup of water, bring to the boil, and cook until the sugar is completely dissolved. Turn the heat to medium and add 2 tablespoons of dillweed, and an 8-ounce jar of French's yellow mustard. Stir well; remove from the heat. Put in a container and refrigerate. Stir well before serving. Place in a bowl to be put alongside the salmon. I prefer to serve this with a crisp cracker. It is really special — the sauce balances the smoky taste of this type of salmon.

*This one I created for a Super Bowl party. I happened to have a side of Northwest smoked salmon left over from Christmas.*

### *How Did I Create This?*

*I began thinking that I would just mix the salmon, cream cheese, horseradish, lemon juice, parsley, and onion powder together to make a simple smoked fish spread. Then I thought it would be interesting to give it an oriental flavor, so I added the teriyaki. Then, I wanted a little unusual crunch, so I added the sesame seeds. Then, I added the sesame oil for a smoky sesame flavor and the brown sugar for just a hint of sweetness.*

### Super Bowl Teriyaki Salmon Spread

I scraped the salmon skin off and pressed paper towels on the fillet to remove the excess oil, crumbled the salmon into a bowl, and added an 8-ounce block of Philadelphia Neufchâtel cheese at room temperature. Then, I beat the 2 of them together with my electric mixer.

Next, I added 1 tablespoon of prepared horseradish, 2 teaspoons of lemon juice, a heaping tablespoon of dried parsley, 1 teaspoon sesame seeds, 2 tablespoons mayonnaise, 1 teaspoon onion powder, 1 teaspoon teriyaki sauce, $1/4$ teaspoon sesame oil, and 1 tablespoon light brown sugar. I beat this with the mixer on high speed — whipping it.

I served it with sesame seeds sprinkled on top. I put sesame crackers out to spread it on. I could have "rolled" it; but, I decided to serve it as a spread. It was quite a hit — there was none left! You could roll this also.

# I Have A Carton Of Sour Cream— Now What?

### Light Mexican Dip

This is a dip I made up for a Vanderbilt tailgate.

| | |
|---|---|
| 1 (16-ounce) carton of light sour cream | ¼ cup finely chopped pimento-stuffed green olives |
| 12 ounces Monterey Jack cheese, shredded | 1 tablespoon finely chopped jalapeños |
| I small can chopped green chilies | 1 teaspoon ground cumin |
| 1 small can chopped black olives | 4 green onions, chopped, or 2 teaspoons dried minced green onions |
| | 1 teaspoon dried cilantro |

Mix well with a spoon. Serve with Tostitos, Fritos, or veggies. It's really good.

### Dip for Grilled Bratwurst or Kielbasa

| | |
|---|---|
| 1 (16-ounce) carton of sour cream | ¼ cup Dijon mustard |
| ½ cup French's yellow mustard | ½ teaspoon white pepper |

Mix well and serve chilled with the grilled sausages.

### Special Soup Mix Dip

When I make that famous Knorr Soup Mix dip, I don't use the water chestnuts and spinach—I use 2 cans of drained and chopped artichoke hearts and 1 small can of sliced black olives instead. Mix with the soup mix and 16 ounces sour cream and serve in a hollowed round of pumpernickel or seeded rye.

### Any-Flavor Soup Mix Dip

Mix sour cream with any dried soup mix for an endless variety of dips for veggies and chips. Don't be timid about using any of them—even split pea or tomato. They are all unique.

*Buck and I have been loyal diehard Vanderbilt sports fans since we were students—eons ago! We have hoped anew with every coaching change that we would have that winning football season. The successes in the basketball program over the years is the only thing that has made football bearable. A couple of years ago, after sitting in the stands and being totally mortified at what the 'Dores didn't do, I went on strike! Actually, now "we" tailgate and "he" goes to the game. More often than not the tailgate is the only party on Saturday.*

## ❧ Notes

*This really is popular with the men – it is a different type of hot dish to serve at a cocktail party.*

• *If using ground beef or sausage, use ground sirloin or Jimmy Dean regular sausage.*

• *For the mushrooms, use fresh and use a combination of several types — white, Portabello, and Cremino are my favorites.*

### Shopping List

*Sausage or ground beef*
*Mushrooms*
*Butter*
*Onion*
*Garlic*
*Dry mustard*
*Hungarian paprika*
*Flour*
*Sour cream*
*White pepper*
*Salt*
*Chopped parsley*
*Melba toast rounds*

## ❧ Chafing Dish Stroganoff ❧

*Of course, sour cream is the ingredient in anything "stroganoff."*

Sauté meats, drain, and rinse under hot water. Set aside.

Mushrooms should be sautéed in a tablespoon of butter until almost dry.

After preparing the meat or the mushrooms, melt 2 tablespoons of butter in a large skillet and sauté 1 large onion that has been finely diced and 4 large cloves of garlic that have been minced. Add 2 teaspoons of Coleman's dry mustard, and 1 tablespoon of Hungarian paprika; stir well.

Toss 2 tablespoons of flour with the meat or mushrooms and add this to the skillet. Add two 16-ounce cartons of sour cream and stir continuously over medium heat until bubbly. Add white pepper and salt to taste. Sprinkle with chopped parsley and paprika before serving. Serve in a chafing dish with Melba toast rounds for dipping.

## ❧ Three More "Chafs" ❧

### Tortellini
For an unusual chafing dish "number," try serving tortellini in Alfredo or plain marinara sauce — serve with toothpicks. You won't get the men to move away from it!

### Barbecue
Another fun thing is to put shredded barbecue in the chafing dish and serve with your favorite barbecue sauce (mine is Bull's Eye) and rolls! I have served it with small corn muffins, but it's a bit messier because the muffin will crumble.

### Sausage Balls
Make small balls out of hot sausage and serve them in warm apple butter or warm applesauce.

# ~≪ Layered Hors D'Oeuvre Cheesecakes ≫~

*Great hors d'oeuvres, that can be made several days ahead.*

## Cheesecake Italiano

First Layer: Mix together 16 ounces cream cheese (not the Neufchâtel; you need cream cheese this time) at room temperature, 4 cloves minced garlic, 4 tablespoons dried thyme, and salt and pepper to taste. Spread in a Saran wrap-lined springform pan and cover completely with fresh basil leaves.

Second Layer: Mix together 12 ounces ricotta cheese, 8 ounces cream cheese at room temperature, 1 tablespoon tomato paste, 4 ounces sun-dried tomatoes, and salt and black pepper to taste. Spread this on top of the basil, covering completely. Chop 8 ounces fresh white mushrooms, toss with the juice of ¹/₂ lemon and 1 teaspoon olive oil, and completely cover the second layer.

Third Layer: Mix together 16 ounces cream cheese at room temperature, ¹/₂ cup crumbled Gorgonzola cheese, 1 small can chopped black olives, and salt and black pepper to taste. Spread this over the mushroom layer. Then chop 1 small bunch of fresh Italian parsley and sprinkle this over the top.

Cover with Saran wrap and put in the refrigerator for up to 3 days before serving. Remove the side of the pan, unfold and remove the Saran wrap. Place on a platter and serve with crackers.

## Marmalade Cheesecake

First Layer: Mix together 16 ounces cream cheese at room temperature, 1 cup grated sharp white Cheddar cheese, ¹/₂ cup finely chopped green onions, 2 teaspoons mayonnaise, and salt and black pepper to taste.

Spread this in a Saran wrap-lined springform pan. Put a layer of toasted finely chopped pecans over the cream cheese mixture.

Second Layer: Mix together 16 ounces cream cheese at room temperature, ¹/₂ jar orange marmalade, and 1 teaspoon orange extract. Spread this over the pecans.

Chill, covered, for up to 3 days before serving. Just before serving unfold and unwrap and place on a platter. Spoon the remaining ¹/₂ jar of orange marmalade on top, sprinkle with chopped chives and a few pecans. Surround with toasted saltine crackers — yes, saltines! Enjoy!

## Zesty Cheesecake

First Layer: You'll need the food processor for this one. Process 4 port wine Cheddar cheese balls at room temperature with 2 tablespoons prepared horseradish. Spread this in a Saran wrap-lined springform pan.

Second Layer: Process 16 ounces cream cheese at room temperature with 16 ounces Saga Blue Danish blue cheese. Spread this over the first layer. Cover the top with chopped chives.

Chill for up to 3 days in the refrigerator. Just before serving unfold and unwrap. Serve with cheese Ritz or plain Ritz crackers.

### Shopping List

*Cream cheese (40 ounces)*
*Garlic*
*Dried thyme*
*Salt and pepper*
*Fresh basil leaves*
*Ricotta cheese*
*Tomato paste*
*Sun-dried tomatoes*
*Fresh mushrooms*
*Lemon juice*
*Olive oil*
*Gorgonzola cheese*
*Chopped black olives*
*Italian parsley*

### Shopping List

*Cream cheese (32 ounces)*
*White Cheddar cheese*
*Green onions*
*Mayonnaise*
*Salt and pepper*
*Pecans*
*Orange marmalade*
*Orange extract*
*Chives*

### Shopping List

*Port wine cheese balls*
*Horseradish*
*Cream cheese*
*Blue cheese*
*Chives*

# Notes

## ~ Some Different Quick Starters ~

### Terrific Toppers for a Block of Cream Cheese

• A.1. steak sauce

• Heinz 57 sauce

• Any chunky salsa

• Chopped shrimp mixed with chutney

### Marmalade And Cheddar

I love to do this at Christmas—spoon orange marmalade over a block of sharp Cheddar. The best Cheddar around is Yukon Gold from Washington State. It's expensive, but I order it every Christmas from Norm Thompson. You can use sharp white Cheddar.

### Hot Stuff

I have even spooned my homemade hot pepper jelly over Cheddar—so-o-o-o good! (For the jelly recipe, see page 139.)

### Chicken-On-A-Cracker

I often put out a bowl of my chicken salad and serve it with Carr's table water crackers. (For the chicken salad recipe, see page 73.)

### Artichokes-To-Die-For

I love fresh artichokes and often serve them as hors d'oeuvres. Serve them with a cold dip made by combining 8 ounces sour cream, 1 teaspoon lemon zest, 1 tablespoon lemon juice, and a few drops of Tabasco Sauce. Or, forget the calorie counters and serve clarified butter—warmed!

*The easiest hors d'oeuvres in the world are created by pouring or spooning something over cream cheese and serving with crisp crackers such as Triscuits.*

### Horsey Crab Meat

Crab meat with a sauce made of 1 cup ketchup, 1 tablespoon lemon juice, 2 heaping teaspoons horseradish, $1/4$ teaspoon ground celery seed, $1/2$ teaspoon onion powder, and—surprise!—1 teaspoon dillweed

### Dijon Marmalade

$1/2$ cup orange marmalade mixed with 1 tablespoon Dijon mustard and $1/2$ cup toasted chopped pecans

*Last Minute: I'm not fond of cocktail party fare that has to be cooked right before serving. However here are a couple of recipes that always bring raves, can be assembled ahead, cooked quickly, and are perfect for "passing around" on trays.*

## Cheese Crab Meat Puffs

Mix together $1/2$ cup of mayonnaise, 8 ounces crab meat (picked over for any bits of shell or cartilage), 8 ounces shredded mild Cheddar cheese, $1/4$ cup grated Parmesan cheese, and black pepper to taste. Spread this, mounding slightly, on toasted baguette slices (crostini). Place under the broiler and broil until puffy. Serve immediately.

This is also wonderful mounded on well-drained and patted dry artichoke bottoms. Depending on their size, you may need to cut them into halves before putting the mixture on and broiling them.

***Shopping List***

*Mayonnaise*
*Crab meat*
*Cheddar cheese*
*Parmesan cheese*
*Pepper*
*Baguettes or artichoke bottoms*

## Olive Pecan Puffs

Mix together 8 ounces cream cheese at room temperature, 1 small can sliced black olives, 1 tablespoon dried parsley flakes, $1/2$ cup chopped toasted pecans, and 2 tablespoons mayonnaise. Spoon this onto Melba toast rounds or into fresh mushroom caps. Bake at 400 degrees for 8 minutes or until puffy. Serve immediately.

***Shopping List***

*Cream cheese*
*Black olives*
*Dried parsley*
*Pecans*
*Mayonnaise*
*Melba toast rounds or mushroom caps*

## Notes

# ❧ Tuscan Treats ❧

*These next recipes are the result of my attempting to duplicate two antipasti we were served in a small charming trattoria that sat, all alone, on a hill overlooking the Tuscan town of Greve in Chianti. They are different and delicious, albeit ones that must be prepared at the last minute. They are both served on crostini.*

To prepare the crostini: Slice a loaf of French bread into 1-inch-thick slices and toast on both sides.

### Sweet Red Onion Crostini

In a large skillet, melt 1 tablespoon of butter and add 1 tablespoon of olive oil. Layer thin red onion slices (2 large onions). Sprinkle sugar over the slices (about $2/3$ cup). Cover and cook over low heat until the onions are limp. Now, pour $1/4$ cup red wine vinegar over the onions and cook over high heat, uncovered, until they are totally wilted and limp and transparent, stirring frequently—but don't let them get brown. Serve immediately, placing a small mound of them on a crostini.

### Tuscan Crostini

In a large skillet, heat 2 tablespoons of olive oil. Sauté 2 cloves of minced garlic and 1 small finely diced red onion. Add 4 or 5 sage leaves, 2 teaspoons of drained capers, a shake or two of black pepper, and 1 pound of drained chicken livers. Cook over high heat, stirring constantly, until the livers are browned and done. Remove from the heat and put in a food processor. Pulse 4 or 5 times —you want a fine chop, not a purée. In the same skillet, melt 2 tablespoons of butter and heat until hot butter is bubbly and foamy. Return the liver mixture to the skillet and cook over high heat for 2 or 3 minutes—until the mixture is just slightly moist. Serve immediately, placing a small mound on a crostini.

*Another wonderful cracker is the one that is served at the Capital City Club in Atlanta. It is served warm and it is wonderful. Try this, 'cause they are really something special.*

# ❧ CCC Crackers ❧

To make CCC Crackers, lightly brush (really dab) clarified butter or butter-flavored oil over Nabisco saltine crackers and toast them under the broiler until they are light brown.

*Last but not least, I promised several folks that
I would include these recipes.*

## ⚞ Homemade Pita Chips ⚟

Cut pita rounds into wedges with kitchen scissors and place on a cookie sheet. Brush with butter and sprinkle with:

- Parmesan cheese, paprika, and oregano;

- Or: Spice Islands Chili Con Carne seasoning, ground cumin, and dried parsley;

- Or: Onion powder, garlic powder, and paprika;

- Or: For low fat, sprinkle the seasonings and then spray the wedges well with Pam and bake as directed.

The combinations are endless! After putting the seasonings on, put them in a 300-degree oven and bake 30 or so minutes until they are well browned. Let cool completely. They will be crisp. They are easy to make and they keep forever in zip lock bags. They are great with any dip or to serve with cheese.

## ⚞ Black-Eyed Pea Salsa ⚟

| | |
|---|---|
| 1 can Bush's from dry black-eyed peas, drained and rinsed | 1 tablespoon dried chives |
| | 1 teaspoon each of ground cumin and dried cilantro |
| 1 can Ro-Tel chopped tomatoes and green chiles, drained | 2 teaspoons Spice Islands Chili Con Carne seasoning |
| 1 can chopped green chiles | 1 tablespoon chopped jalapeño (optional) |
| 1 tablespoon dried minced onion | |

Simply combine everything at least 2 hours before serving. Serve with tortilla chips or Homemade Pita Chips — that's the other recipe.

**Notes**

# Breakfast and Brunch

Although I almost never eat breakfast now, when our sons were living at home, we always had big breakfasts! When they were teenagers I would fix — every Saturday — 2 pounds of bacon, 1 pound of sausage, 1½ dozen scrambled eggs, grits, hash browns, and cinnamon rolls or biscuits. Whew!

Then on Sunday, it was 2 pounds of bacon, pancakes or waffles or French toast, and sometimes sautéed apples. Our youngest, John, loved chocolate chips in his waffles or pancakes.

I usually used Bisquick Mix to make the pancakes and waffles, but I would mix it the night before and refrigerate it — and I used 1 more egg than the recipe on the box called for, and I used melted butter instead of oil in the waffle recipe.

And yes, I did make those Sunday Night Waffles (page 40) every now and then!

## Two Famous Biscuits

*There are two biscuit recipes I am going to share with you — both from well known places that sell a lot of biscuits.*

### Famous Cafe Biscuits

The first one is from a wonderful cafe that's just down the road a way. This cafe makes biscuits people "love" to eat. Needless to say, if you use this recipe you can have them anytime.

Measure 2 cups self-rising flour into a bowl. Add a small carton of whipping cream and mix with a fork until a ball forms — you may need to add more liquid — the ball should be slightly wet. If you do need to add any more, add it a drop at a time. And you can add milk if you don't have any more cream. (If this happens to me, I put a little milk in the cream carton and shake it and use this.) Roll out on a floured surface and cut into biscuits. Brush with melted butter and bake at 400 degrees until brown.

## Biscuits That Made Mrs. Winners Famous

Buck was President and CEO of Winners Corporation from 1980 until 1986. At that time, Winners Corporation was the largest Wendy's franchisee and owned Mrs. Winners Chicken and Biscuits. The biscuit recipe was a copy of Bojangles biscuit—which was considered, at that time, to be the best biscuit in the business. A Winners executive was somehow able to get the secret Bojangles recipe and they were off and running trying to perfect it.

Buck must have made a thousand in our kitchen! Yes, Buck. He was and is a believer in the saying "experience is the best teacher." He attended Wendy's Management School and he worked in a store actually doing everything the employees did—from cooking to cleaning.

He worked at every possible position in the Mrs. Winners stores from cutting the chickens, to making the biscuits, to cleaning the chicken fryers and replacing the oil. He believed that he should know the operation inside and out. He required every executive to do the same and they all did this again and again for one week every year as long as they worked for the company. He always believed that all the employees were a part of "The Team." And the better he and the other executives knew what each and every member of the team did and had "hands on" experience in every job, the better the team would be.

This is the original biscuit recipe—it is a big fluffy buttermilk biscuit and is incredibly easy to make. Buck still makes them every Christmas. You will get messy because you mix the dough by hand.

| | |
|---|---|
| **2 pounds Crisco solid shortening** | **1 gallon buttermilk** |
| **10 pounds self-rising flour** | **melted butter** |

Buck reduces these measures to 1, 5 and $1/2$ for our use. Cut the shortening into the flour with a pastry cutter or two knives. Add the buttermilk a little at a time, mixing it into the flour with your hands—this is a very "wet" biscuit dough. Put the dough—$1/2$ at a time—on a well-floured surface. Sprinkle the dough with a little flour and roll out to desired thickness. Cut into biscuits and place them on a greased baking sheet. Brush with melted butter and bake at 400 degrees for 10 to 12 minutes or until brown. Brush with melted butter again immediately after taking them out of the oven.

*For Old-Fashioned Baking Powder Biscuits, see page 40.*

*This is wonderful if you use raisin bread or other types of nut or sweet yeast breads. Cake types fall apart in the egg mixture.*

## ✥ French Toast ✥

6   **eggs, beaten until frothy**
1   **cup milk**
1   **cup half-and-half**
1   **teaspoon vanilla extract**
1   **teaspoon orange zest (optional)**

¼   **teaspoon cinnamon**
1   **tablespoon butter**
1   **tablespoon Crisco oil**
**Bread slices**

Mix eggs, milk, half-and-half, vanilla, zest, and cinnamon together. Heat 1 tablespoon butter and 1 tablespoon Crisco oil in a skillet. Dip bread slices in the egg mixture—submerging. Put the bread slices in the skillet and fry, turning to brown both sides. Do not crowd the skillet. You will need to add butter and oil each pan full. Serve with powdered sugar or heated syrup. Yum!

## ✥ Sawmill Gravy ✥

Sometimes, I make sawmill gravy, mixing flour and water (instead of milk) and adding it to the sausage drippings left in the skillet—doing exactly like Peggy taught me to make any gravy with flour. I use approximately the same amount of flour as drippings and mix the flour with twice the amount of water as flour. A delicious addition is a chopped tomato—don't do this with anything but ripe summer tomatoes. There's nothing better to me than gravy and Peggy's biscuits.

## ✥ Homemade Doughnuts ✥

A neat thing to do with biscuits from a can. Put a hole in the middle and stretch to make the hole big. Fry in hot Crisco oil until brown and roll in powdered sugar.

# Cinnamon Swirl

*Any biscuit dough shouldn't be reworked more than once.*
*It will become "tough." The Cinnamon Swirl was created to take*
*care of this "tough" dough.*

Put the scraps left from cutting the biscuits into a pile and form them into a ball. Roll this into a rectangle and sprinkle very generously with a mixture of sugar and cinnamon — 2 parts sugar to 1 part cinnamon. Sprinkle with raisins that have been soaked in warm water and drained and roll up. Chill the dough so slicing will be easier. Slice into $1^{1}/_{2}$-inch slices. Bake at 400 degrees until done. Spread the frosting on while hot.

The frosting is made by combining powdered sugar with milk or water — 2 to 4 tablespoons of milk or water to 1 pound powdered sugar and adding 1 teaspoon vanilla extract. It is really more of a glaze.

*While I'm at it, I'll share another fast-food secret.*

# Pretty Close To Wendy's Chili

To make a chili that will come pretty close to tasting like Wendy's, add $^{1}/_{2}$ jar of Mexene chili powder and 2 tablespoons of dried minced onion to 2 pounds of ground chuck that you have browned and drained and rinsed in hot water to get rid of the grease. Next add a 24-ounce can of crushed tomatoes and two 15-ounce cans of small red beans — not kidney beans. Cook as you usually cook chili — simmering for 2 to 3 hours.

Wendy's uses really good fresh ground beef for their burgers. The burgers are made fresh every day and never "carried over" to the next day. This is the same meat that goes into the chili. They boil it and rinse it to remove any grease. (They use burgers that have either fallen apart while they were being cooked on the grill or extra patties that were not grilled that day.)

After the meat is drained, it is chopped into pieces no bigger than a dime. Then the onions and chili seasonings and crushed tomatoes and "little red beans" are added. It is good stuff.

# Brunch #1

*This really easy menu will serve 8 to 10 and can be prepared ahead.*

## ~ Different Sausage Pinwheels ~

I make sausage pinwheels using Pillsbury All Ready Pie Crust instead of bread dough or biscuit dough. Spread 1/2 roll of sausage (I use Jimmy Dean Sage or Hot) on each crust. Roll up and cut into 1/2-inch slices. Place slightly apart on a baking sheet and bake in a 350-degree oven until brown — about 25 minutes. Remove them from the baking sheet to cool slightly. Serve warm.

## ~ South Carolina Cheese Pie ~

*My version of a very old recipe I got from South Carolina. Absolutely decadently wonderful!*

1/2 pound each ricotta cheese, Feta cheese, Muenster or Monterey Jack cheese, and Gruyère or Swiss cheese
12 eggs, well beaten

1 pound butter, melted
1/4 teaspoon each black pepper and nutmeg
18 sheets filo pastry

Crumble or grate the cheeses together (you will have 2 pounds total). Beat the eggs together. Mix in 1 cup of the melted butter. Brush the remaining 1 cup butter on each of the 18 filo sheets. Place 10 of them in an 11x14x2-inch baking dish. Pour the cheese mixture in the pan, and put the remaining 8 filo sheets on top. Bake in a 350-degree oven for 30 to 35 minutes or until golden brown. Let cool slightly before cutting into squares.

*Brunch is an easy and usually less costly way to entertain. Serve them all with assorted breads, sweet muffins or scones, and/or biscuits.*

# Brunch #2
### *This menu will serve 8.*

# Eggs Baked In Tomatoes With A Special Hollandaise

8 large tomatoes
8 artichoke bottoms
1 stick butter, melted

8 large eggs
salt and pepper to taste

## For the hollandaise:

2 eggs
8 ounces Philadelphia
   cream cheese
3 tablespoons fresh lemon juice

¹/₄ teaspoon each salt and white
   pepper
1 can crab meat, drained and
   rinsed and picked over

Wash and cut the tops off the tomatoes, scoop out the pulp, and turn upside down to drain on paper towels. Butter an 11x14x2 baking dish and place the artichoke bottoms in the dish. Brush the artichoke bottoms with melted butter, and put the tomatoes on top of them. Spoon 1 teaspoon of melted butter in each tomato. Break 1 egg in each, and sprinkle with salt and pepper. Place the dish in a 350-degree oven to bake for about 30 minutes—or until the eggs are done to your liking. While they are cooking, make the hollandaise.

Beat eggs into the cream cheese one at a time, beating well after each one. Add the lemon juice and the salt and pepper; beat well. Stir the crab meat into the sauce and put the sauce in the top of a double boiler. Set over hot, but not boiling, water. Cook, stirring constantly, until the sauce is thick and fluffy.

To serve: After taking the eggs from the oven, gently slide a spatula under each artichoke bottom and lift onto individual plates. Ladle the warm crab meat hollandaise over the top and serve.

# Broiled Grapefruit Halves

You will need ¹/₂ grapefruit per person. Cut around the inside of the grapefruit and between the sections, so that the grapefruit will be easy to eat. Sprinkle dark brown sugar on top, be generous, and press. Preheat the broiler in the oven. Place the grapefruit on a baking sheet and place on the oven rack closest to the broiling element. Broil until the sugar has bubbled and slightly caramelized—watch closely. Serve immediately.

## ⁓ Menu

*Sour Cream Quiche*
*Frozen Tomato Salad*
*Baked Apples*

# Brunch #3
### *This menu will serve 8 to 10.*

## ⁓ Sour Cream Quiche ⁓
### *This recipe makes 2 quiches. I love this recipe,*
### *it does not have the usual crust.*

| | |
|---|---|
| 8 eggs, well beaten | 3 tablespoons chopped chives |
| 16 ounces sour cream | 1 tablespoon chopped parsley |
| 8 ounces Monterey Jack cheese, shredded | 1 teaspoon each black pepper and thyme |
| 8 ounces Swiss cheese, shredded | 10 slices Virginia Baked Ham or 1 pound bacon that has been |
| 2 small cans sliced black olives | cooked, but is still limp |

Beat the eggs. Add the sour cream, cheeses, olives and the seasonings; mix well. Spray two pie pans with Pam and lay the ham or limp bacon slices in the pans, overlapping and placing so that the sides and bottom are totally covered. Pour the egg mixture in, dividing equally. Put the pans in a 425-degree oven. Bake for 12 minutes. Then, turn the heat down to 375 degrees and bake until the filling is set, about 25 or 30 minutes. Let sit for 3 to 5 minutes before cutting into wedges. This will serve 8 to 12 people depending on the size of the wedges.

### A Mexican Variation: Olé!

| | |
|---|---|
| 8 eggs, well beaten | 1 teaspoon onion powder |
| 16 ounces sour cream | $1/4$ teaspoon Tabasco sauce |
| 6 ounces Monterey Jack cheese, shredded | 3 tablespoons dried chives |
| 2 small cans chopped green chiles | $1/2$ teaspoon cumin powder |
| 1 teaspoon dried cilantro | 2 Pillsbury ready-bake pie shells |

Mix eggs, sour cream, cheese, chiles, and seasonings together and pour into two unbaked pie shells. Bake at 425 degrees for 10 minutes. Turn down to 375 degrees and bake until set. Serve this with a dollop of sour cream and fresh salsa and black bean garnish — rinse a can of cooked black beans and either use as a garnish on top of the salsa or mix with the salsa and use that way.

• *I love the fresh salsas by Strickland's Supreme Salads — they are in the produce section.*

• *Serve this Mexican version with the Avocado Grapefruit Salad (page 75) and grilled Choriso sausages.*

# ☙ Frozen Tomato Salad ❧

### *I love this one, too.*

| | |
|---|---|
| 1 (28-ounce) can crushed tomatoes | ¹/₂ teaspoon Tabasco Sauce |
| 1 tablespoon onion powder | salt and black pepper to taste |
| ¹/₂ teaspoon ground celery seed | 1 cup of Kraft mayonnaise |

Put all of this in a blender and blend on high until smooth. Put this in a 9-inch square pan that you have sprayed lightly with Pam. Cover with Saran and freeze.

To serve: Cut into squares and place on a piece of red leaf lettuce or radicchio. Put a dollop of mayonnaise that has been mixed with a little Tabasco Sauce — ¹/₄ teaspoon to 1 cup mayonnaise.

# ☙ Baked Apples ❧

### *This also works well with acorn squash halves.*

You will need 1 apple per person or ¹/₂ acorn squash per person. Core the apple, but don't go all the way through. If using squash, clean out the center. Mix together butter, nutmeg, allspice, and vanilla, making a paste—for 1 stick of butter, use ¹/₂ teaspoon nutmeg, 1 teaspoon allspice, and 1 teaspoon vanilla extract. Put 1 tablespoon in each apple, pushing it as far as it will go. Use 2 tablespoons in each squash. Fill the rest of the apple with Karo dark corn syrup. Add 2 tablespoons to each squash. Place in a Pam-sprayed baking pan. Bake in a 375-degree oven for 30 minutes for the apples and 40 minutes for the squash.

To serve: Place on a plate and sprinkle with chopped, toasted pecans or walnuts.

## Notes ❧

*When I was growing up in Atlanta, Mana, my cousin Judy, and I would eat lunch at Brookhaven Country Club every now and then. They made this and served it on a "trio salad plate" with either chicken or tuna salad and potato salad. I decided a few years ago that I would love to taste it again. Well, since all I had to go on was remembering, it took quite a few tries. To my taste buds this is pretty close to it.*

### *Shopping List*

*Apples or acorn squash*
*Butter*
*Nutmeg*
*Allspice*
*Vanilla extract*
*Karo dark corn syrup*
*Pecans or walnuts*

# ≈ Eggs Ormond ≈

• *Another unique thing to do for brunch — make a seafood version of eggs Benedict! Put a poached-egg on a Crab Cake and serve with warm Rémoulade Sauce spooned over it. Really good!*

• *This is a Bays Build a Better Benedict Contest Prize Winner.*

| | |
|---|---|
| 8 ounces lump crab meat | 1 tablespoon drained capers |
| 1/3 cup plain bread crumbs | flour for dusting |
| 2 tablespoons mayonnaise | 1 tablespoon extra-virgin |
| 1/8 teaspoon cayenne pepper | olive oil |
| 1 teaspoon Dijon mustard | |

Pick over the crab meat, removing any shell and cartilage you may find. Mix the next 5 ingredients together and form into 4 loose cakes. Dust the cakes with flour on both sides. Sauté the cakes in 1 tablespoon of extra-virgin olive oil to brown both sides. When brown, place on a greased baking sheet and put in a 350-degree oven for 10 to 15 minutes to finish cooking the cakes.

## Make A Rémoulade Sauce

| | |
|---|---|
| 1 cup mayonnaise | 1 tablespoon minced scallions |
| 3 tablespoons Dijon mustard | (tops only) |
| 1/8 teaspoon each ground celery seed, cayenne pepper, and white pepper | |

Mix all together. To serve warm, heat in a double boiler.

Poach 4 eggs. Remove the crab cakes from the oven.

To assemble the dish, you will need:

| | |
|---|---|
| 1 Bays English Muffin half per person (2 for hearty appetites) | 1 poached egg |
| | salt and pepper to taste |
| | warm Rémoulade sauce |
| 1 thick slice of tomato | chopped parsley, scallions, and |
| 1 crab cake | capers for garnishing |

Place 1 Bays English Muffin half on each plate. Place the tomato slice on the muffin. Next, place the crab cake on the tomato and the poached egg on the top. Season with salt and pepper to taste. Spoon the warm Rémoulade Sauce over all. Garnish with some chopped parsley, scallions, and a few capers. Serve accompanied by fresh steamed asparagus with lemon butter sauce.

# ⤛ Chicken Salad Á La Rawls ⤜

6 chicken breasts, boiled until
   done, then diced
4 ribs celery, diced
½ cup slivered almonds
2 tablespoons each dried chives
   and dried parsley

salt and pepper to taste
2 teaspoons Durkees sauce
enough Kraft mayonnaise to
   moisten (½ to ¾ cup)

Combine all in a bowl. Mix well with a fork. It's really a hit! Try serving as an appetizer, too.

When I was 12 years old, Momma and Daddy let me ride on the bus downtown with friends to see a movie. Things were quite different back then in Atlanta in 1956. I'm sure they wouldn't have let me if it were now, and probably wouldn't have from the late 1960s to now. But, back then, Momma would take me to Buckhead where I would meet a girl friend and we would get on the bus . It would let us out in the front of Loew's and we would see the matinee. Then, we would eat a little late lunch, and catch the bus back to Buckhead where our mothers would pick us up.

*Salads—I eat one every day. I remember the delicious Pineapple Cream Cheese Salad that Momma used to make. And the wonderful chicken salad that I used to eat at Leb's Delicatessen in Atlanta. And the one I used to eat at the Quick and Tasty Restaurant in Ormond Beach Florida —I love 'em!*

*I loved to eat at Leb's Deli which was just a block or so farther down Peachtree Street from Loew's. I would always order the chicken salad on a rye roll and strawberry cheesecake. To this day, I haven't tasted any chicken salad that's better. Mine is similar, but I add almonds.*

## ✎ Notes

*Did you know that if an egg "floats" when put in water, it isn't fresh?*

*Also, hard-boiled eggs are easier to peel if they are allowed to cool in the water they were boiled in and then put in cold water before peeling. Always crack the large end first to break the air pocket. The shell will come off easily.*

## ✎ Egg Salad—Deli Style ✎

This is an all-time comfort food. Hard boil 6 eggs. Coarsely chop and mix with enough Kraft mayonnaise to be glumpy. Then add 1 teaspoon Durkees sauce and salt and pepper to taste. Mix with two forks—sort of "toss."

## ✎ Stuffed Eggs ✎

Since we're talking about eggs, let's stuff some.

Cut 6 hard-boiled eggs in half, remove the yolks, and mash the yolks with 1 teaspoon of Durkees Sauce, 1/2 teaspoon sweet pickle juice, and enough mayonnaise to moisten—1 or 2 tablespoons. Add 1/2 teaspoon salt and 1/4 teaspoon pepper. Mix well and restuff the whites. Sprinkle with paprika. I sometimes garnish with a slice of pimento-stuffed olive, too. Serve cold.

*There was a restaurant in Ormond called the Quick and Tasty. Absolutely bar-none, the best seafood place that ever was!*

*We went to Ormond Beach, Florida, for a month every summer. Daddy would drive us down and fly back to Atlanta, fly back down and drive us back. He only got to spend a few days with us at each end. Ormond Beach is just about 10 miles north of Daytona Beach. Anyway, back then—in the "olden days," Daddy always ordered flounder, Momma had scallops and we kids had shrimp. With every order, you got a salad, bread, and either baked potato or French fries. The salad was very simple and I guess that's what made it so delicious.*

## ✎ The Q-T Salad ✎

In each small salad bowl, place shredded iceberg lettuce. Put a couple of slices of fresh tomato on top of that. Then put about 1/4 cup of finely diced celery. Sprinkle 1/4 teaspoon of onion powder over the celery. Lastly, drizzle 1 tablespoon of Crisco oil over it, followed by a little bit more than 1 teaspoon of white vinegar. Do not toss. Serve and let each person use salt and pepper to their taste. So good!

# ~≪ **Avocado Grapefruit Salad** ≫~

*2 grapefruit and 2 avocados will make salad for 6.*
*Wonderful and pretty year 'round.*

In the winter use fresh grapefruit. In the time of the year that fresh isn't available, use the grapefruit in jars that you find in the refrigerated section of your market's produce department. Select ripe avocados, peel, cut in half, and slice. Place the slices on a platter. Arrange the grapefruit on the plate. Spoon the following dressing over all and serve.

**Dressing:**

| | |
|---|---|
| ¹/₂ cup sugar | 1 teaspoon each salt and |
| 1 tablespoon each paprika, |    Lawry's seasoned salt |
|    celery seed, poppy seed, | ¹/₄ cup cider vinegar |
|    and dry Colman's | 1 cup of Crisco oil |
|    English Mustard | |

Process sugar, seasonings, and vinegar in a blender on high. Drizzle the oil in slowly while blending.

# **Spinach Salad With Mandarin** ~≪ **Oranges And Walnuts** ≫~

*The perfect thing to serve with anything Mexican*
*or with pork or with seafood.*

Remove the stems from 2 bunches of fresh spinach leaves. Clean and rinse the leaves and dry them. Put the leaves in a large salad bowl, cover, and keep chilled until serving time. Just before serving, drain 2 small cans of mandarin oranges and scatter them over the spinach. Scatter 1 cup of toasted walnut halves over everything. Drizzle the dressing over and toss.

• *The dressing for the Spinach Salad With Mandarin Oranges And Walnuts is the same dressing I use on the Avocado Grapefruit Salad.*

• *To toast nuts: place the nuts on a baking sheet and put in a preheated 275-degree oven. Watch closely and remove when they are toasted.*

# ≈⊱ Toasted Pecans ⊰≈

At Christmas, it is a tradition in our house to always have a bowl of toasted, buttered pecans out to munch on. This is an easy thing to do. Put the pecans in a shallow pan. Pour melted butter over the pecans — use 1 stick for 3 pounds of pecan halves. Sprinkle a small amount of salt over the pecans. Using a spoon and spatula turn the pecans over and over to make sure all are coated. Put in a 250-degree oven and bake for about 30 minutes, turning them over once or twice more. They are addictive!

# ≈⊱ Anne's Cold Coleslaw ⊰≈

Buck's mother, Anne, makes wonderful slaw. She makes a dressing out of $3/4$ cup mayonnaise, 3 teaspoons yellow mustard, 1 tablespoon sugar, 1 teaspoon vinegar, salt and pepper to taste. She mixes this well and pours it over 4 cups shredded cabbage, 1 finely minced onion, 1 finely shredded carrot , and $1/2$ finely chopped green pepper. She mixes this well and serves it chilled, sprinkled with paprika. Serves 6.

# ≈⊱ A Trio Of Tomatoes ⊰≈

### With Mozzarella And Basil

Slice the tomatoes and arrange on a serving platter with fresh basil leaves and fresh mozzarella cheese slices in this order: tomato, basil, cheese, tomato, basil, cheese and so on until all are arranged. Drizzle extra-virgin olive oil over and sprinkle with a little bit of salt and freshly ground pepper.

### With Spinach And Blue Cheese

Use fresh spinach leaves instead of the basil and Saga Blue Danish blue cheese instead of the mozzarella. Arrange in the same way, drizzle the olive oil and 1 or 2 teaspoons of balsamic vinegar, too. Finish with the salt and freshly ground pepper.

### With Pasta

For this one, coarsely chop the 4 large tomatoes and mix with 1 tablespoon of balsamic vinegar, 1 tablespoon red wine vinegar, and 5 tablespoons extra-virgin olive oil. Toss this with 1 small jar of drained capers and 8 fresh basil leaves that you have chopped. Mix well and spoon over 1 pound of your favorite pasta — I love angel hair for this.

*• In the summer, when tomatoes are so good, I have three favorite things to do with them for salads. First, drop the tomatoes in boiling water and leave for 30 or 40 seconds — the skin will slip off. Peel and core the tomatoes and turn upside down on paper towels to drain.*

*• Four tomatoes and 12 ounces of cheese will make 8 servings.*

# ⤸ One More Pasta Salad ⤸

## For the dressing

Combine in a small bowl and set aside: 1 bottle of Lawry's Red Wine—with Cabernet Salad Dressing, and 3 minced garlic cloves, 1 tablespoon onion powder, $1/2$ cup extra-virgin olive oil, and $1/2$ cup malt vinegar.

## In a large bowl put:

| | |
|---|---|
| 2 cans artichoke hearts, drained and quartered | 12 ounces cheese such as farmers, Monterey Jack, or fresh mozzarella that you cube |
| 8 ounces fresh mushrooms, sliced | |
| 1 carton cherry tomatoes, washed and cut in half | 10 fresh basil leaves, coarsely chopped |
| 1 bunch green onions, chopped | 1 pound cooked pasta (I use tricolor fusilli.) |
| 1 small can sliced black olives | salt and freshly ground pepper |

Toss all of this with the dressing ingredients you set aside. Season with salt and freshly ground black pepper. Serves 10 to 12.

# Thompson's
# ⤸ Seedless Grape Salad ⤸

Clean 4 pounds of seedless grapes, remove them from the stems and dry them. Mix together 8 ounces Philadelphia cream cheese, $1/2$ cup cream, and 1 tablespoon Miracle Whip salad dressing. Combine the dressing and the grapes. Serve cold. This dressing would be great on other fruits. And you might try adding some chopped nuts! Serves 6.

*I made this from what I happened to have on hand to take to a tailgate party. It will make a huge bowl full.*

*Try this and think about what you could make from things you have on hand—you can do it!*

## Notes

# Some Salad Dressings

### Ann's

My Aunt Ann, Momma's sister, makes a great one from scratch. She puts some oil and cider vinegar in a bowl — approximately $1/3$ cup vinegar to $1/2$ cup oil. Then, she puts about 1 teaspoon yellow mustard and 1 tablespoon ketchup, and salt and pepper to taste. Then, she stirs it like crazy with a fork and pours it on.

### Peggy's

Peggy made another one. In a bowl, put 2 tablespoons paprika, 2 teaspoons salt, $1/4$ teaspoon cayenne pepper, $1/4$ teaspoon black pepper, $1/4$ cup ketchup, the juice of 1 lemon, $1/4$ cup cider vinegar, and $2/3$ cup Crisco oil.

### Rawls' Vinaigrette

Whisk together in a bowl: 1 teaspoon balsamic vinegar, $1/2$ teaspoon Lea & Perrins Worchestershire sauce, $1/4$ cup red wine vinegar, $1/2$ teaspoon each salt and pepper, 2 minced garlic cloves, and $2/3$ cup of olive oil.

### Rawls' Fresh Salsa Dressing

For a different twist, mix one container of Strickland's fresh salsa — mild or medium — with $1/4$ cup lemon juice, $1/4$ cup white vinegar, 1 tablespoon dried cilantro, and 1 cup olive oil. Really good!

# Joe's Stone Crab Sauce

*This would be good on any seafood salad.*

| | |
|---|---|
| 1  cup mayonnaise | 1  teaspoon A.1. sauce |
| $1/8$ cup heavy cream | $2^{1}/_{2}$ teaspoons Colman's dry |
| 2  teaspoons Lea & Perrins |     mustard |
|     Worchestershire sauce | dash of salt |

Mix all ingredients together in a blender.

*This one is great on fruit and, of course, any seafood! It is the secret (until now) from Joe's Stone Crab in Miami!!!! This is really it!!*

# ❧ The Best Tuna Casserole ❧

2 (7-ounce) cans tuna, drained and rinsed under hot water
16 ounces cottage cheese
16 ounces sour cream
1 medium onion, chopped
2 tablespoons dried parsley
1 teaspoon each Lea & Perrins Worchestershire sauce and Durkees sauce
1 tablespoon lemon juice
16 ounces fettucine, cooked
Parmesan cheese

Mix the tuna with the cottage cheese, sour cream, onion, parsley, and seasonings. Mix this with the cooked fettucine. Put in a greased casserole dish and top with a generous layer of Parmesan cheese. Place in a preheated 350-degree oven and bake for 30 minutes. Serves 6 to 8.

# ❧ Sutherland Casserole ❧

Patricia and Pete Sutherland are the only couple I know who started going steady in kindergarten, continued through high school, got pinned in college, and are still married — a grand total of 45-plus years! They are the parents of three lovely women. The youngest, Susan, is our godchild. They are the godparents of our son Michael. They are special friends. This is their version of shepherd's pie.

1 pound ground round
1 large onion, chopped
2 Idaho baking potatoes, diced
1 (8-ounce) can each sweet peas, carrots, lima beans (a total of 3 cans)
1 (15-ounce) can of kidney beans, drained
1 (6-ounce) can of tomato paste
1 (14-ounce) bottle of ketchup
salt and pepper to taste
1 (8-ounce) can creamed corn

Brown the ground round and add everything else except the creamed corn; mix well. Cook over low heat for 1 hour, stirring often. Now, add the creamed corn. Cook for an additional $^1/_2$ hour. Serves 6 to 8.

• I guess every cook has a million or more recipes for casseroles—well, at least some anyway. These are some that I have especially liked and my family enjoyed—even the two picky eaters who "don't like things all mixed together."

• I won fifth place in a cooking contest for this recipe.

## ❧ Notes

*My mother-in-law, Anne, is a very good cook. She bakes wonderful yeast rolls. She makes awesome pot roasts and beef briskets. Her cabbage slaw is the best anywhere. She bakes delicious pies and her fresh coconut cake is to die for! Each of my sons is lucky enough to get a whole one all to himself each birthday. Her turkey tetrazzini is the best I've had, and here it is…*

# ❧ Anne's Turkey Tetrazzini ❧

| | |
|---|---|
| ½ cup chopped onions | 6 cups grated sharp Cheddar cheese |
| ½ cup chopped celery | |
| 8 tablespoons butter | ½ cup Parmesan cheese |
| 5 tablespoons flour | 12 ounces spaghetti noodles, cooked |
| 1 (8-ounce) can mushrooms, drained | |
| 2 cups milk | 4 cups chopped cooked turkey |
| 2 cans condensed cream of mushroom soup | 2 cups crushed saltines or Ritz crackers |
| 2 cloves garlic, minced | 1 cup broken pecans |

Sauté the onions and celery in half the butter. Add the flour and stir. Add the mushrooms and the milk. Cook until thickened, stirring constantly. Add the mushroom soup, garlic, and the cheeses. Stir well and combine with the cooked spaghetti and the turkey.

Add the remaining butter, melted, to the cracker crumbs. Put the turkey mixture in a long flat casserole dish; sprinkle the cracker crumbs and then pecans on top. Put in the oven and bake at 350 degrees for ½ hour. Watch closely the last few minutes so the crackers and pecans don't burn. Serves 8 to 10.

# ❧ Escalloped Corn ❧

### *This is an old recipe and a good one.*

| | |
|---|---|
| 1 (15-ounce) can creamed corn | 1 cup half-and-half or cream |
| 1 cup of crushed Ritz crackers | salt and pepper to taste |
| 2 eggs, beaten | butter |

Mix the first 6 ingredients together and pour into a buttered casserole dish. Dot the top with butter and bake for 30 minutes in a 350-degree oven.

# Vidalia Onion
## And Mushroom Casserole

*I created this for a dinner party and was so pleased with the
way it turned out, I actually wrote it down!*

8  ounces fresh mushrooms,
   sliced
4  large Vidalia onions, thinly
   sliced
¼ cup butter
16 ounces sour cream
12 ounces Monterey

Jack cheese, shredded
¾ cup shredded Parmesan
   cheese
2  eggs
2  teaspoons Tabasco sauce
salt and pepper to taste

Place the sliced mushrooms in a casserole dish. Put in a 350-degree oven and bake until dry.
Sauté the onions in the butter until they are just limp. Add them to the mushrooms and toss well.
Mix the other ingredients and pour over the mushroom/onion mixture; mix well. Put in the oven
and bake at 350 degrees until done — 35 to 40 minutes. Turn the broiler on to brown the top if
needed. Serves 10.

## Pineapple Perfect

2  (15-ounce) cans pineapple
   chunks, drained
½ cup packed brown sugar
8  ounces sharp Cheddar cheese,
   shredded

1  roll of Ritz crackers, crushed
1  cup pecan pieces
1  stick butter, melted

Mix the pineapple with the brown sugar and put in a casserole dish. Sprinkle with the cheese, the
crushed crackers, and the pecans. Drizzle with the butter, making sure you moisten the whole top.
Bake at 350 degrees for 30 minutes or until hot and browned on top.

## ℐ Notes

*Buck and I visited Italy for two wonderful weeks with our dear, dear friends, Carol Ann and Joe Pryor. We had an incredible time and we ate incredible food. We all were captivated by the regional flavors — the subtle additions and slight changes in the food — as we moved from Venice in the Northeast, to Bologna in the middle, to Rome in the South, to Tuscany — Florence, Siena, Bagno A Ripoli, Monteriggioni — and finally to Bellagio on Lake Como in the North at the foot of the Italian Alps.*

# ⊰ A Sauce Or Four ⊱

### A Simple Tomato Sauce

Sauté 2 finely minced garlic cloves in 1 tablespoon of olive oil over medium heat, stirring constantly for about 1 minute. Do not sauté over high heat because garlic burns very quickly and burned garlic is awful! Add 4 coarsely chopped fresh basil leaves and sauté this for a few seconds. If it's not summer and fresh tomatoes aren't available, use a 28-ounce can of plum tomatoes (I use Progresso). Chop them and add them and their juice. If you can get fresh ones, peel and chop 8 or so and add them. Stir and lower the heat to simmer. Cook for 20 minutes or so and serve over al dente pasta, tossing the pasta with the sauce just before serving. Pass the Parmesan! Enough for 1 pound of pasta.

This is the sauce I use on my pizzas.

### Alfredo Sauce

For 1 pound of pasta, melt 1 stick of sweet butter in a large skillet over medium heat. Add 12 ounces of heavy cream and cook, stirring constantly, until it thickens — about 4 or 5 minutes. Add a twist or two of freshly ground pepper (I use black here, not white) and a sprinkle of salt. I usually add about 1 cup of grated Parmesan now and stir until it's melted. I pour the sauce over fettucine, toss well and serve with a sprinkling of Parmesan. Delicious!

Try adding an 8-ounce can of backfin crab meat to the Alfredo—Fabulous!

*The use of things like butter, cream, olive oil, garlic, eggs, seafood, meat, seasonings, and even tomatoes, changed with each region. All were used, but in different proportions.*

*It was fascinating! And it presented a new set of challenges for me — to use these things that I learned — adapting and adjusting the Italian recipes that I already have, and, of course, hopefully, creating new ones. Since we've been back, I've been having a blast trying new dishes and re-inventing old favorites. Now, I'm sharing them all with you!*

## All-Purpose Meat Sauce

Sauté 2 pounds ground chuck in a skillet. When done, drain and rinse meat in a colander under hot water to remove the grease. Put the drained meat in a large deep pot and set aside.

Now, in a skillet, sauté one finely chopped large onion and a finely chopped garlic clove in 2 tablespoons olive oil until limp and transparent. Add this to the meat.

Add 1 cup of red wine and cook over medium-high heat, stirring to prevent any sticking. Now add two 28-ounce cans of crushed tomatoes and one 28-ounce can of tomato purée. Add 1 large and 1 small can of tomato paste, 2 tablespoons each of sugar, basil, and parsley, and 1 tablespoon each of oregano and thyme. Add 2 bay leaves, 1 teaspoon of salt, and 1 teaspoon of pepper. Cook this on simmer, stirring every so often for 2 hours.

It can be used now, but I always make it at least a day before I plan to use it and refrigerate it until I do use it—it gets better.

## White Clam Sauce

Sauté 4 minced garlic cloves in 2 tablespoons of olive oil. Add $\frac{1}{4}$ cup of chopped parsley, 2 cans of chopped clams, and 2 cups of white wine. Cook over high heat for 2 or 3 minutes, stirring constantly. Serve immediately over pasta. Easy and quick. Enough for $\frac{1}{2}$ pound of pasta.

*Always when I make this sauce to use in lasagna, I remove the casings from 1 pound of mild Italian sausage and sauté it along with the ground chuck.*

*Don't forget to discard the bay leaves.*

*I add 1 small can of tomato sauce and use red wine instead of white to make red clam sauce.*

## ✑ Notes

*These are two lasagnas, "before" and "after" Italy.
There are sixteen layers in one and seventeen in the other—
these are lasagnas that cry for a party!! Have 'em both.*

• *If you do use the aluminum foil pans, Please Be Sure To Place The Pan On A Cookie Sheet Before You Put It In The Oven To Cook. This Is A Weighty Dish!!*

• *For All-Purpose Meat Sauce, see page 83.*

## ⤛ Before Italy Lasagna ⤜

The recipe for this lasagna was given to me in 1970 by Carol Ann Pryor. I have modified it some over the past 27 years, but it is essentially the same. This was the only recipe for lasagna that I ever used before our Italian trip.

The pan I use for this is the bottom of a rectangular turkey roaster. It is 6 inches deep and is the only pan I have that is big enough. I have used the aluminum foil pans that you can buy in the grocery store, making sure that I buy the extra-deep ones. This recipe makes enough to serve at least 16. If I have any leftovers, I cut into individual servings and wrap each in Saran and aluminum foil, freeze and have them on hand for quick dinners to just unwrap and zap in the microwave.

For these lasagnas, I make my Meat Sauce recipe using 2 pounds of ground chuck and 1 pound Italian sausage. And, I always make it the day before I make the lasagna. It has to be cool before you can assemble the lasagna, so this works well for me.

Ingredients you will need in addition to the meat sauce ingredients:

| | |
|---|---|
| 2 (1-pound) boxes lasagna noodles | ¼ cup dried parsley |
| 24 ounces ricotta cheese | 1 teaspoon black pepper |
| lots and lots of Parmesan cheese | 2 pounds mozzarella cheese (I use slices) |

You will need to parboil 2 boxes of lasagna noodles for 6 minutes or so, drain, rinse well, and lay flat on kitchen towels—clean, of course. If you don't, they stick together and are virtually impossible to get apart without tearing them apart! I haven't tried the "no cook" lasagna noodles yet, so I can't recommend them. But, feel free to use them and let me know how it works!

Now, with the sauce and noodles ready, you need to combine 24 ounces of ricotta cheese with $1/2$ cup of Parmesan cheese, $1/4$ cup of dried parsley, and 1 teaspoon of black pepper. Set aside.

Grease your pan with olive oil, and begin layering:

1. Spread a small amount of sauce in the bottom of the pan
2. Layer 4 noodles across
3. Layer 4 mozzarella cheese slices
4. Spread a layer of sauce
5. Layer 4 noodles
6. Layer 4 mozzarella cheese slices
7. Spread all the ricotta cheese
8. Sprinkle with Parmesan cheese
9. Spread a layer of sauce
10. Layer 4 noodles
11. Layer 4 mozzarella cheese slices
12. Spread a layer of sauce
13. Layer 4 noodles
14. Spread a thin layer of sauce
15. Layer 4 mozzarella cheese slices
16. Sprinkle lots of Parmesan cheese on top!

This needs to bake for $1^1/2$ hours in a 350-degree oven—covered for the first hour. Uncover the last $1/2$ hour, so the top can get bubbly and brown. Let it sit for at least 15 minutes before cutting into squares to serve. Serves 12.

*I serve this with a simple salad, Boboli Wedges (page 53), and a good Italian Chianti. It is well worth the effort to make—it is always wonderful!*

**Notes**

*For All-Purpose Meat Sauce, see page 83.*

# ❧ After Italy Lasagna ❧

The lasagna we ate in Italy was lighter and seemed to have endless layers. They don't put a lot of sauce or cheese between the pasta layers and they always use a Béchamel sauce—either as the only sauce, or combined with a simple tomato sauce or a Bolognese meat sauce—a ragoût. This classic sauce from Bologna contains ground beef (chuck), pork, and sometimes veal. The meat is sautéed in butter along with chopped onion, carrots, and celery. It also contains chopped Italian plum tomatoes, a little wine, and sometimes milk that is added to cut the acidity of the tomatoes. Some lasagnas are made with the ragoût and Béchamel combined to make one sauce. I use the meat sauce that I usually make and I also make a Béchamel sauce. I don't combine them; I alternate them when I layer the lasagna.

## Béchamel Sauce

A cream sauce just like the "basic" cream sauce that I watched Peggy make for so many years. Peggy made a medium-thick sauce. For the lasagna, the sauce needs to be a little thinner—so I add a little more milk.

| | |
|---|---|
| 2  sticks sweet butter | 1  cup flour |
| 9  cups whole milk, heated | 1/2  teaspoon salt |

In a large saucepan, melt the butter. Add 7 cups of the heated milk. Mix the flour and salt with the remaining 2 cups hot milk, stirring until there are no lumps—it will be pasty. Add the flour mixture to the hot milk in the saucepan and cook over medium heat until it is thick, stirring constantly. The sauce needs to be cooled to room temperature before assembling the lasagna.

O.K., you have the meat sauce, and the Béchamel Sauce is made and cooled. Now, cook the 2 boxes of noodles for 6 minutes just like you did in the first lasagna recipe, rinsing and laying on clean towels.

The rest of the ingredients you will need are:

| | |
|---|---|
| lots of a Romano/Parmesan mix made of 1 part shredded Romano mixed with 2 parts shredded Parmesan | 16 ounces ricotta cheese (not 24) 2  pounds mozzarella cheese |

Mix 2 tablespoons of the Romano/Parmesan mix with the ricotta cheese.

Grease your pan with olive oil, and layer the ingredients:

1. Spread a thin layer of Béchamel Sauce in the bottom of the pan

2. Sprinkle with Romano/Parmesan

3. Layer 4 noodles

4. Spread a thin layer of meat sauce

5. Layer 4 mozzarella cheese slices

6. Layer 4 noodles

7. Spread a thin layer of Béchamel Sauce

8. Sprinkle with Romano/Parmesan

9. Layer 4 mozzarella cheese slices

10. Spread all of the ricotta thinly

11. Sprinkle with Romano/Parmesan

12. Layer 4 mozzarella cheese slices

13. Layer 4 noodles

14. Spread a thin layer of meat sauce

15. Layer 4 noodles

16. Layer 4 mozzarella cheese slices

17. Spread a generous layer of the Béchamel Sauce and put a lot of the Romano/Parmesan on it

Cover with foil and bake at 350 degrees for 1 hour. Uncover and bake for ¹/₂ hour longer. Let it sit for 15 minutes before cutting. I really think that this is the best lasagna I have eaten. Serves 12.

## Notes

- *With either of these lasagnas, if you divide the work and spread it over a couple of days, they are really easy and fun to assemble. And wonderful to serve!*

- *The basic meat sauce can be used over any pasta — except angel hair which is too delicate for any heavy meat or cream sauce.*

## ❧ Notes

*A little over 10 years ago, there was an Italian restaurant on West End Avenue that specialized in pasta and pizza—J.D. Double Crust. They had really unique Chicago-style pizzas with loads of cheese and lots of toppings and their specialty was a double crust pizza! The toppings were inside the pizza and the sauce and cheese were on top of the second crust—it was sort of a pie. I thought that it would be fun to try at home. So, there I go again — creating and having fun!*

# ❧ A Stuffed Italian Pie ❧

### *It is wonderful served at room temperature —I take it often to tailgate parties.*

| | |
|---|---|
| 2 pounds hot Italian sausage, casings removed | 1 (10-ounce) package of frozen chopped spinach, thawed |
| 2 (28-ounce) cans crushed tomatoes | 2 eggs |
| 2 (8-ounce) cans tomato sauce | 1/2 teaspoon pepper |
| 2 (6-ounce) cans tomato paste | 1/2 cup grated Parmesan cheese |
| 2 cloves of garlic | pizza dough |
| 1 medium onion, chopped | olive oil |
| 1 teaspoon each dried oregano, basil, parsley and thyme | 1 pound each of sliced provolone and sliced mozzarella cheese |
| 1/2 teaspoon fennel seeds | 1 package of sliced pepperoni |

Sauté the sausage, crumbling it well. Drain and rinse. Set aside. In a blender, put the tomatoes, sauce and paste, plus garlic, onion, herbs and fennel seeds. Purée. Put this purée and the sausage in a saucepan and cook on low heat for 3 to 4 hours—it has to be thick. Squeeze all of the moisture out of the spinach by placing it in a towel and wringing it. Combine the spinach with the 2 eggs that you have beaten. Add pepper and Parmesan cheese; mix well.

## *I combined a whole lot of different Italian things that I liked and came up with this version.*

If you are using the Pillsbury dough, put one in a well greased springform pan–stretching it so it forms to the pan and overlaps the edges. Brush olive oil all over the crust. Layer the filling as follows:

| | |
|---|---|
| 1. Half the provolone slices | 5. All the spinach |
| 2. Half the sausage sauce | 6. The mozzarella slices |
| 3. Half the mozzarella slices | 7. The sausage sauce |
| 4. All the pepperoni | 8. The provolone |

Put the second crust on top of this and bring up the overlapping bottom crust pieces and seal the edges by crimping. Place in a preheated 500-degree oven for 10 minutes. Turn the heat down to 400 and bake for 40 minutes. Let it cool to room temperature before cutting into wedges. You need not take the pie out of the springform pan.

If using My Pizza Crust, fit half the dough into the pan. Brush the dough with olive oil and layer. Serves 10.

# ❧ My Pizza Crust ❧

### *This recipe makes 2 large crusts.*

I make mine in my food processor. I proof the yeast first in a glass measuring cup. I put in 1/2 cup of warm water and stir in a pinch of sugar. Then, I put in 2 packages of Fleischmans yeast, and in a few minutes it will start to foam if the yeast is alive — if it doesn't foam after 8 or 10 minutes, throw it out and start again.

Place 5 cups of bread flour in the bowl of the processor along with 1 1/2 teaspoons of salt. Process to mix. With the machine running, pour in the yeast mixture, 2 1/2 cups of warm water and 2 teaspoons of olive oil. You may need up to 1/2 cup more of water and/or 1/2 cup of flour, depending if the dough is too dry or too wet — don't add it if you don't need to. Let the dough sit in the processor for 2 minutes and then, process again for 1 minute. Do this one more time.

Now, turn the dough into a large bowl that has been wiped with olive oil. Cover the bowl with a clean kitchen towel, set in a warm place, and let rise until it has doubled.

Divide the dough in half and begin to manually stretch the dough with your fingers. You can do this in a greased pizza pan. You will have to let it rest periodically.

To assemble the pizza, brush the dough with olive oil, spread the tomato sauce on, put any topping you like on now, and finally, sprinkle with mozzarella or Provolone cheese. Place in a preheated 500-degree oven on the bottom shelf and bake until brown and bubbly.

# ❧ Pizza Dough ❧

I make my own pizza dough, but you can use two of the Pillsbury pizza crusts that are in tubes in the dairy case at the grocery. For that matter, you could use two of the Pillsbury French bread dough.

I would use Boboli Crusts for a pizza party because they will cook faster — and, you cook them one at a time. Or, you could use the small Boboli and do individual ones so you can cook several of the small ones at a time.

*I have a baking stone that covers the bottom of my oven. I put the stone in the oven 30 minutes before baking and preheat the stone at 500 degrees. I also cook my pizzas directly on the stone, using a peel dusted with cornmeal to slide the pizza onto the stone. Our favorite is plain cheese with fresh basil leaves placed on the sauce.*

### *Party Time*

*Have a make-your-own pizza party. Give each couple their own crust and let them make their own from ingredients you have set out in bowls. Put out the sauce, cheese, and toppings such as green peppers, mushrooms, sliced pepperoni, cooked Italian sausage. You could even put out pesto sauce for "white" pizzas, and feta or gorgonzola, and assorted "up town" ingredients for "gourmet" pizzas. Serve beer, wine, and a big salad. It's a good, casual, fun party.*

*John Henderson and Buck were in the same Fraternity, Kappa Sigma, at Vanderbilt. We have been friends since then. He is a member of The "Tailgate Team" — actually, I think he was the originator of the group. He and Buck go to the games — I don't anymore, but then, you already know that. John is a stockbroker and he loves crossword puzzles — he and Buck are crossword puzzle freaks! One more thing, he is a really good cook. He has shared three of his specialties — all family secrets — with me, so, you get to have them, too. They are Mother Henderson's Potato Soup (at right), Mother's Baked Beans (page 95), and his "World Famous" Chili (page 94).*

*Try adding a can of crab meat or baby shrimp that you have drained and rinsed.*

# Mother Henderson's
## Potato Soup

| | |
|---|---|
| 2$^1/_2$ cups water | 3$^1/_2$ tablespoons flour |
| 2 cups diced potatoes | 1$^3/_4$ teaspoons salt |
| 2 onions, minced | $^1/_8$ teaspoon pepper |
| 2 outside ribs of celery with leaves, diced | 2 cups milk, scalded |
| 3 tablespoons butter | 1 tablespoon finely chopped fresh parsley |

Boil the water and add the potatoes, onions, and celery. Cook until very tender. Melt the butter in the top of a double boiler. Add the flour, the seasonings except the parsley, and stir until smooth. Add the hot milk and cook until smooth, stirring constantly. Run the potato mixture through a strainer, rubbing the solids; it should yield about 3 cups of purée. Mix the purée with the thickened sauce and serve sprinkled with the parsley.

# A Famous Artichoke Soup
### *This is a delicious soup!*

| | |
|---|---|
| 2 (10-ounce) cans artichoke hearts, drained | 2 egg yolks |
| 3 cups of chicken stock | 3 tablespoons flour |
| 2 cups half-and-half | 2 tablespoons lemon juice |
| 1 cup heavy cream | salt and pepper to taste |

Place the artichoke hearts, chicken stock, half-and-half, cream, egg yolks, and flour in a blender and purée. Place in a saucepan and cook until the soup is thickened and bubbly, stirring constantly — do not boil. Add lemon juice and salt and pepper and reheat and serve. Delicious hot or cold.

# Notes

## ≈ Beans and Bean Soups ≈

Back in the 60s and early 70s, there was a restaurant in Green Hills, where the Green Hills Grille is now, called Nero's Cactus Canyon. They were famous for their hot water corn cakes and white bean soup. They were famous for other things also, but Buck loved those two the most. When Nero's closed, Buck had a time finding another white bean soup that was as good. Then he tried the soup that is served at Richland Country Club. Eureka! He found it! Anyway, a few years ago, he decided that he would devise a white bean soup of his own. It's a very good soup.

### Buck's White Bean Soup

Soak 1 pound of Great Northern beans overnight. Drain the beans and set aside. In a large stockpot put about 10 cups of water and a fatty piece of leftover country or "city" ham or 2 or 3 pieces of bacon. (We usually have some scraps of country ham or some Honey Baked Ham in the freezer left from Christmas. I use ham pieces year-round to flavor greens and beans.) After the meat has cooked for 30 minutes, add 1 finely diced onion, 3 finely chopped carrots, a 28-ounce can of crushed tomatoes, 1 or 2 tablespoons of Tabasco sauce (or to taste), and salt and pepper to taste. Let this simmer for at least 3 hours, stirring frequently. Serve it with cornbread or corn cakes and more Tabasco sauce.

*For Hot Water Corn Cakes, see page 108.*

*Buck has added chopped summer sausage — you know, the kind that comes in the gift packs you always get at Christmas. This really makes the soup a meal in itself.*

### *Shopping List*

*Dry Great Northern beans*
*Ham or bacon*
*Onion*
*Carrots*
*Canned tomatoes*
*Tabasco sauce*
*Salt and pepper*

*I have often joked that we joined the club for the soup first and golf second.*

**Notes**

### Esther Validos' Cuban Black Beans And Black Bean Soup

When Buck was president of Winners Corporation, Dave Champion was in charge of the Advertising Department. Dave and his wife, Esther, became friends of ours, and we got to know both of their families. Esther's mother, Mrs. Validos, was one of the nicest people I ever knew. She was of Cuban ancestry. When she cooked Spanish and Cuban foods, you knew it was the real thing. She gave me this recipe for Cuban Black Beans. I include my variation that makes it soup.

| | |
|---|---|
| 1 **pound black beans, wash and let soak overnight in enough water to cover** | 1 **onion, finely chopped** |
| | 4 **cloves of garlic, mashed (I use a garlic press)** |
| 3 **bay leaves** | ½ **cup olive oil** |
| 1 **tablespoon vinegar** | ¼ **cup tomato sauce** |
| 1 **green bell pepper, finely chopped** | |

*Don't forget to discard the bay leaves.*

After soaking, put the beans on high heat and bring to the boil. Add the bay leaves and vinegar. Lower the heat to medium. Sauté the bell pepper, onion, and garlic in the olive oil. Add to the beans along with the tomato sauce. Cook for 2 to 3 hours on low until they are thickened and soft. Serve over rice.

### Rawls' Black Bean Soup

Add a 28-ounce can of crushed tomatoes, and increase the tomato sauce to 1 cup. Add ½ teaspoon of ground cumin and 1 teaspoon of oregano, and salt and pepper to taste. Serve with croutons, chopped green onions, Tabasco sauce, and Parmesan cheese.

### White Beans Tuscany-Style

Soak 1 pound white beans in water overnight. Drain the beans and add fresh water to the pot — barely cover the beans. Add 2 mashed cloves of garlic and ¼ cup of olive oil. Cook the beans over medium-low heat for 1½ hours. Just before serving, sauté 6 chopped sage leaves, 2 minced garlic cloves, and 4 diced tomatoes in ¼ cup olive oil. Pour this over the hot beans, stir and serve.

# ⮜ Chili—Three Different Versions ⮞

### Orgasmic Chili

Sound intriguing? Well, it is good chili. It was christened that by a dear friend, Ed Vance. Ed and his wife, Carole, were eating a chili supper at our house a few years back on a very cold February night. Ed remarked that the chili was the best he had ever eaten—that it was so good, "It is orgasmic."

| | |
|---|---|
| 3 pounds ground chuck, cooked, drained, and rinsed under hot water | 1 teaspoon Hershey's cocoa powder—not sweet |
| 2 onions | 2 tablespoons paprika |
| 4 cloves of garlic | 2 teaspoons each oregano and onion powder |
| ¼ cup Chili Con Carne seasoning | 1 teaspoon sugar |
| 1 tablespoon ground cumin | salt and pepper to taste |

After the meat is cooked and rinsed, put it in a large stockpot. Put all of the other ingredients in a blender and purée. Add to the pot. Now, add:

| | |
|---|---|
| 1 (28-ounce) can of crushed tomatoes | 2 tablespoons Wyler's granulated beef bouillon |
| 1 (28-ounce) can tomato purée | |

Let this cook for 4 or 5 hours over low heat, stirring occasionally, and tasting for salt and pepper seasoning adjustments. I do not like to add things like masa or cornmeal to thicken my chili. I am not fond of the consistency or flavor it imparts—however slight it may be.

I do not add beans directly to my chili—I put them in a separate bowl along with bowls of chopped onions, shredded Cheddar cheese, and Parmesan cheese for people to mix with the chili as they desire. Serve with Aunt Callie's Cornbread—you might even agree with Ed!

*If I do not have the luxury of 4 or 5 hours to cook the chili, I add a small can of tomato paste after 2 hours of cooking if it has not thickened enough.*

*For Aunt Callie's Sour Cream Cornbread, see page 108.*

**Notes**

*Don't forget to discard the bay leaf.*

### "World Famous" Chili

This is the second of three recipes that our friend John "Mudge" Henderson shared with me.

| | |
|---|---|
| 3 pounds ground beef | 2 teaspoons Worchestershire |
| 1 large onion and green pepper, both chopped | sauce |
| 3 tablespoons oil | 2 dashes of Tabasco sauce |
| 1 clove of garlic, crushed | 2 or 3 hot peppers, such as jalapeño or serano or |
| 2 cans diced Rotel tomatoes | cayenne (optional) |
| 1 (8-ounce) can tomato sauce | approximately 2 teaspoons salt |
| 1 bay leaf | and 1 teaspoon pepper or to |
| 1 or 2 tablespoons chili powder | taste |
| 1 tablespoon ground cumin | 1 (30-ounce) can chili beans |
| 1/3 cup ketchup | |

In a Dutch oven, brown the ground beef and drain any fat off. At the same time, in a small skillet, sauté the onion and the bell pepper in the oil. Add this and all the other ingredients — except the beans — to the meat. Simmer for several hours. Just before serving, add the beans.

### Gourmet Club 5-Way Chili

This recipe is from my folder of recipes from a couples' Gourmet Club that we belonged to about 15 years ago. Sadly, it disbanded after two of the couples in the club "split" — one "split town" and one just "split." Different chili, but good.

| | |
|---|---|
| 3 large onions, chopped | 1 small can of tomato paste |
| 2 cloves of garlic, chopped | 1 teaspoon each cumin, red pepper flakes, garlic salt, |
| 1/4 cup oil | and pepper |
| 2 1/2 pounds ground chuck | 1/4 cup chili powder |
| 4 cans beef bouillon | 2 teaspoons salt or to taste |
| 1 (28-ounce) can crushed tomatoes | 2 (15-ounce) cans of kidney beans |
| 1 cup Heinz ketchup | |

Sauté the onions and garlic in the oil. Add the beef and sauté. Then add all but the beans. Simmer for 2 hours or longer if desired. Just before serving, add the beans.

*What makes it 5-way?*

*Eat it as is.*

*Serve over spaghetti.*

*Top with chopped onions.*

*Sprinkle with sharp Cheddar cheese.*

*And you think of other ways.*

# Beans Beans Beans — Baked Baked Baked
## Three ways to bake beans

### Mother's Baked Beans

The third recipe from John Henderson. He cooks them in a cast-iron Dutch oven — maybe that's his secret. Anyway, they are really good.

| | | | |
|---|---|---|---|
| 1 | large onion, finely chopped | 2 or 3 | dashes of Tabasco sauce |
| 1 | green pepper, finely chopped | 1/2 | cup ketchup |
| 4 | (15-ounce) cans pork and beans | 1 | cup (about) packed brown sugar |
| 2 | teaspoons Worchestershire sauce | | bacon slices for the top |

Sauté the onion and green pepper in a little oil in the Dutch oven. Add the undrained beans and the seasonings; stir well. Sprinkle about 1 cup of brown sugar over the top and lay a few slices of uncooked bacon over the brown sugar. Bake at 400 degrees for 45 to 60 minutes. Watch closely so it doesn't get dry.

### Pat's Baked Beans

Our friend, Pat Gray, gave me this recipe many years ago. They are very rich and very good.

| | | | |
|---|---|---|---|
| 1 | pound sausage, your preference as to hot or mild | 1/2 | cup packed brown sugar |
| 2 | large onions, finely chopped | 1 | tablespoon Lea & Perrins Worchestershire sauce |
| 3 | (28-ounce) cans pork and beans | | salt and pepper to taste |
| | | 1/2 | pound bacon |

In a large skillet, sauté the sausage and onions together — don't drain. Add the beans, brown sugar, Worchestershire sauce, salt and pepper to taste, and the Tabasco sauce. Put in an oblong baking dish and lay the bacon on top. Bake at 350 degrees for 1 to 1 1/2 hours — don't let them get dry.

*If not using hot sausage, add 1/2 teaspoon Tabasco sauce.*

## Notes

### Famous Recipe Beans

These beans are my adaptation of the baked beans served at some of those famous chicken places—No, not Mrs. Winners!

| | |
|---|---|
| 3 (28-ounce) cans pork and beans | ¼ cup liquid smoke |
| | 2 tablespoons dark Karo Syrup |
| 3 large cans of Sloppy Joe sauce | 5 or 6 bacon slices, cut up |
| 2 tablespoons dried minced onion | 1 jar Hormel real bacon pieces |

Drain the beans and mix with the Sloppy Joe sauce. Add the rest except the bacon pieces and mix well. Put in a greased baking dish and scatter the bacon pieces evenly on the top. Put in the oven and bake for an hour or so—don't let it get too dry. If it starts to dry out, take it out of the oven—it will be done. They do taste good—not too sweet and not too spicy.

## ⤙ Hoppin' John ⤚

### *Hoppin' John is a real Southern dish. Serve with turnip greens and cornbread and pass the Tabasco sauce! Yum-m-m-m!*

I start by soaking 1 pound of dried black-eyed peas in water overnight. The next day, I put a couple of nice pieces of ham—country or "city"—in a large pot filled ³/₄ full with water. Bring the water to the boil, turn the heat down and simmer for about 30 minutes. Then add the drained peas, 2 tablespoons onion powder, 1 teaspoon ground celery seed, 1 teaspoon Tabasco sauce, ¼ cup cider vinegar, 1 teaspoon Lea & Perrins Worchestershire sauce, 1 teaspoon sugar, and 1 teaspoon pepper. Don't add salt yet. Let this simmer together for 2 hours, stirring occasionally. After the 2 hours, add 1 teaspoon salt and ³/₄ cup of rice and stir. Let this simmer, covered, for 20 minutes. After 20 minutes, remove the cover and check to be sure it isn't dry. Add hot water a little at a time as needed—Hoppin' John is not soupy or dry, it's just moist. Replace the cover and simmer until the rice is done—about 10 or 20 more minutes.

*Shopping List*

*Dried black-eyed peas*
*Ham*
*Onion powder*
*Ground celery seed*
*Tabasco sauce*
*Cider vinegar*
*Worcestershire sauce*
*Sugar*
*Pepper*
*Salt*
*Rice*

# ❦ Oysters And Wild Rice ❦

### *I always serve scalloped oysters at Thanksgiving. I don't use oyster crackers when I layer the dish; I either use small seasoned croutons or wild rice.*

*For Peggy's Perfect Rice, see page 33.*

Rinse 8 ounces wild rice under warm water. Put the rice in a small pot and add enough water to cover by at least 1 inch. Cook the rice for 15 minutes—it will not be completely done. Drain the rice and put all of it in the bottom of a round 2- or 3-quart casserole dish. Drain 3 pints of select oysters. Put the oysters on top of the rice. In a saucepan, put 16 ounces heavy cream and 1 tablespoon Lea & Perrins Worchestershire sauce, 1 teaspoon Tabasco sauce and heat to the simmer—don't boil. Dot the top of the oysters evenly with 1 stick of butter. Pour the cream over all; add more cream if it doesn't cover the oysters. Put in a 375-degree oven and bake for 45 to 60 minutes. This is so-o-o-o good!

***Note:*** Cook the rice in chicken or beef stock—it adds great flavor without adding fat.

### *Shopping List*

*Wild rice*
*Oysters*
*Heavy cream*
*Worcestershire sauce*
*Tabasco sauce*
*Butter*

## *My all time favorite way to eat rice was with a lot of Peggy's fried chicken gravy on it—now, that was real comfort food! Yes, ma'am!*

# ❦ Suzita's Authentic Mexican Rice ❦

My grandmother, Mana, went out to California every summer to visit her relatives from her Father's side of her family, the Drakes. She, Momma, and Ann would spend lots of time with "Cousin Gene" and "Cousin Frances." Suzita was their live-in Mexican housekeeper and cook. Momma, Mana, and Ann agreed that she made tamales from heaven. I think that was pretty close to the only time they ever agreed on anything! Regrettably, that is not the recipe I have—I'm not sure that that one was ever written down. The recipe that I have is for a delicious Mexican version of Spanish rice.

- **1 cup rice**
- **3 tablespoons oil or bacon drippings, if you have them**
- **1 medium onion, finely diced**
- **1 small clove of garlic, mashed**
- **1 small can of tomato sauce**
- **2 tablespoons salt (I use 1 or 2 teaspoons)**
- **2½ cups water**

Wash and drain rice. Heat the oil or drippings in a deep pan. Put the rice in and cook until the rice is a golden brown, stirring constantly. Add the onion and the garlic. Let fry, but don't let it get brown. Add the tomato sauce and stir to blend. Add 1 teaspoon of salt and the water. Stir over high heat until it comes to the boil. Turn the heat down to simmer. Put the lid on the pan and don't take it off for 45 minutes. Then remove the lid, but don't stir because you will have mush instead of rice. Serve after it has sat for 5 minutes.

# ~ Meat Loaf ~

*My three sons' favorite meat loaf. Serves 6 to 8 with mashed potatoes, green beans, macaroni and cheese, and rolls. It's yummy!*

Cooking for three boys and a husband could get pretty expensive. For instance, if I had fried chicken for dinner, I had to fry 2 chickens plus 4 extra breasts — and I still only got the wings for myself. If I had a roast, I cooked 2 chuck roasts. If I had spaghetti, I cooked 2 pounds of spaghetti noodles. If I had hamburgers, they each had at least 2. And the killer was breakfast: 2 pounds of bacon or 2 pounds of sausage, at least 20 biscuits, 18 eggs, and they drank 1 gallon of milk a day!

None of them was ever overweight — they were "growing boys." Since ground beef was one of the most economical meats to buy, I used a lot of it. They ate hamburgers, Salisbury steak, meatballs, meat sauce, tacos — but not meat loaf. I tried every recipe for meat loaf that I found. They wouldn't eat any. Then I decided that I would combine the things that I knew they would eat and come up with, hopefully, a meat loaf even they would eat. All three of my sons love the way this meat loaf tastes. Even now, they either request this meat loaf, lasagna, or Peg's fried chicken when they bring their families over for dinner.

When they all come, it's a total of 12 counting Buck and me! As I'm in the kitchen preparing, I always have a sense of "been there, done that." Except now it's more like "I've been there and I can't believe I'm doing this again."

2$\frac{1}{2}$ pounds ground chuck
$\frac{1}{4}$ cup dried minced onion
6 tablespoons Wyler's beef bouillon granules
1 teaspoon each salt, pepper, sugar, and dried parsley
2 eggs
2 cups rolled oats (you may need $\frac{1}{2}$ cup more)
1 can condensed cream of mushroom soup

Simply dump everything in a large mixing bowl and, with your hands, mix it all very well — it will be very mushy. If it seems to be too loose to hold any shape, then add the extra $\frac{1}{2}$ cup oats. Dump it in a large rectangular pan and shape it into a loaf. Place in a 375-degree oven. Bake for 30 minutes. Then turn the oven up to 425 degrees and bake for 15 minutes — this makes the outside crispy. Let it sit for about 7 minutes before slicing.

# ✒ The Best Chuck Roast ✒

### Let me assure you—I will never cook a chuck roast any other way!

This recipe actually was the result of a mistake I made. I was planning my grocery list and had decided to fix a chuck roast for one night's dinner. I usually used a package of Lipton onion soup mix and a can of condensed Campbell's cream of mushroom soup to season my roast—sprinkling the onion soup on the roast and then spreading the soup over that. I didn't check to be sure that I had the mushroom soup (I always had at least one can of mushroom soup in the pantry). Well, as I was preparing the roast to go into the oven, I discovered that I didn't have any. Now what?

I looked in the pantry and I did have a packet of dry Hidden Valley Ranch dressing. So I sprinkled both the onion soup mix and the dry ranch dressing mix over the roast, wrapped it in foil, and baked it at 350 degrees for $2^1/_2$ to 3 hours like I always do. It is the moistest roast imaginable and the gravy that it makes as it cooks is delicious. My personal motto has always been "if you get handed a lot of lemons—simply make lemonade," and this time I made some really good stuff! Try it, I know you'll like it too.

# ✒ Stroganoff For Company ✒

| | |
|---|---|
| 1 **small onion, grated** (I use the food processor) | 2 **tablespoons each dried chives** and dried parsley |
| 3 **cloves of garlic, minced** | $1^1/_2$ **pounds thinly sliced round** or sirloin steak strips |
| 4 **tablespoons butter** | $1^1/_2$ **pints sour cream** |
| 2 **tablespoons Brandy** | $^1/_4$ **teaspoon nutmeg** |
| 2 **teaspoons Columan's dry** mustard or Grey Poupon Dijon mustard | **salt and pepper to taste** |

Sauté the onion and the garlic in butter. Add the Brandy, the mustard, the chives, and parsley. Add the meat and stir until the meat is done. You can prepare it to this point up to a day ahead. Just before serving, add the sour cream and heat through, but don't boil. Stir in the nutmeg and salt and pepper to taste. Serve over buttered noodles or rice and sprinkle with fresh chopped chives or parsley for presentation. It's a classic dish. What makes mine a little different is the mustard. Serves 8.

• *Serve over buttered wide noodles, or I like to serve it over wild rice. Use sliced round or sirloin steak—or go all out and substitute strips of tenderloin and really impress!*

• *For Stroganoff for hors d'oeuvres, see page 58.*

*Mr. Smith was kind enough to share this recipe with me about 25 years ago. Buck and I were having cocktails at his home, and we were served this as an appetizer. I remarked that I would love to know how he made the spiced beef. A few days later, I received this recipe in the mail. I was thrilled and have made it many, many times. It is a lot like Spiced Round, but I like it much better.*

*I make a pork barbecue that everyone thinks I bought. It really is better than any I've ever bought and Nashville has quite a few good barbecue places. Try it for yourself.*

*This recipe and I were included in an Anne Byrne article in* The Tennessean *in January 1995.*

# Mr. Fleming Smith's Spiced Beef

| | |
|---|---|
| 1 ounce (¹/₈ cup) each ground ginger and saltpeter (I buy it at a drugstore) | 1¹/₂ teaspoons ground cloves |
| | 1 (4- to 5-pound) flank of beef (I buy flank steak) |
| 2 tablespoons each pepper and allspice | 6 tablespoons salt |
| | ¹/₂ cup sugar |
| 1 tablespoon ground nutmeg | 1 cup water |

Combine the saltpeter and spices (except for the salt and sugar). Rub both sides of the beef, using all the mixture. Place the beef in a glass pan and sprinkle the salt and sugar on top. Cover with Saran wrap and place in the refrigerator for 2 weeks—turn every day. After 2 weeks, remove the beef and roll it in as tight a roll as you can. Wrap it with cheesecloth and tie it. Place the roll in a roasting pan with 1 cup of water. Cover the pan and roast the beef in a 325-degree oven for 2¹/₂ to 3 hours. Serve the beef very cold and sliced in paper thin slices, cutting against the grain.

# Barbecue Made At Home That Tastes Like You Didn't

| | |
|---|---|
| 1 (5- to 6-pound) pork roast— Boston butt | 4 to 6 tablespoons Cavender's Greek seasoning and onion powder |
| 1 bottle liquid smoke | |
| 1 small bottle Tabasco sauce | |

Turn your gas grill on high and put the roast fat side down on the grill to sear. It will begin to flame and smoke. Carefully turn the roast over and sear the other side. When seared on both sides, remove (and remember to turn the grill off). Place the roast fat side up on a large sheet of heavy-duty aluminum foil—spray the foil with Pam first. Pour ¹/₂ of the bottle of liquid smoke evenly over the roast; shake ¹/₂ the bottle of Tabasco sauce evenly over the roast. Now, sprinkle the roast with enough Cavender's to completely cover the surface of the roast. Lastly, sprinkle with the same amount of onion powder. Wrap the roast tightly in the foil and put it in a roasting pan. Place the pan in a 275-degree oven. Bake for 6 or 7 hours. After cooking, unwrap and remove the roast from the pan. Remove the bones and fat from the roast, and shred the meat— I use two forks. Serves 6 to 8.

# A Simple Roasted Pork

### Either a loin roast or a fresh ham.

Make slits in the meat and put slivers of garlic in them. Rub the roast with ground sage and rosemary. Rub the roast with olive oil. Place in a greased roasting pan and roast at 450 degrees for 10 minutes. Turn the heat down and roast for 15 or 20 minutes a pound at 350 degrees or until a meat thermometer reaches at least 170 degrees.

# My Way To Cook Country Ham

### It's moist and not too salty and slightly sweet.

Soak the ham in water overnight. Wash the ham and remove any mold with a stiff brush. Place the ham in a pot big enough to hold the ham and the cooking liquid. I use a large turkey roaster. I cook the ham in a mixture of 1 liter bottle of 7-Up, 1 cup white vinegar, $1/2$ cup honey, $1/2$ cup packed brown sugar, and enough white wine to cover. Let this simmer for 30 minutes a pound. Cover and let the ham cool in the liquid. Remove the ham, take the skin and fat off of it. Refrigerate. Serve the ham thinly sliced on biscuits.

# Baked Ham That Is Always Yummy

Place the ham cut side down on a sheet of heavy-duty aluminum foil that has been sprayed with Pam. Gather the foil up around the ham. Pour over the ham one or a combination of the following: regular Coca-Cola, regular Mountain Dew, apple juice, or Gatorade. Enclose the ham in the foil and seal. Place the ham in a pan and put in a 325-degree oven. Bake for 30 minutes a pound. When done, don't unwrap — let the ham completely cool before you open the foil. After cooling and removing from the foil, you will be ready to eat a ham you'll love!

# A Sunday Night Ham Sandwich

Spread two slices of rye bread with mayonnaise and Durkees sauce. Place a slice of mozzarella cheese on both slices. Then, put a slice of ham on one slice and cover the ham slice with a generous portion of drained sauerkraut. Place the other bread slice cheese side down over the sauerkraut. Melt some butter in a skillet and grill the sandwich on one side; turn over, add more butter, and grill the other side. Continue turning until it is golden brown on both sides.

# Some Other Things I Like
## To Do With Meats

• Sprinkle freshly ground pepper and Cavender's Greek seasoning on steaks or burgers or pork chops before grilling.

• I promise this is not hot! Sprinkle freshly ground pepper and 1 or 2 teaspoons of Tabasco sauce on burgers before they are grilled.

• Make a ketchup-based barbecue sauce, using Del Monte ketchup — it is made with pineapple vinegar and pineapple juice contains papain, a natural tenderizer.

• When grilling steaks, rub a cut clove of garlic all over the meat, brush with olive oil, and sprinkle with freshly ground black pepper on both sides before grilling. You'll be making Costata Alla Fiorentina, Florentine steaks. In Italy, this is done with large T-Bone steaks, that are ample for 2 or 3 people and they are served very rare. They almost "moo"!

• Another "good thing" to do to burgers and steaks before grilling them is brush them with Kitchen Bouquet; it really gives them a great flavor and I swear it seals the juices in! When I do this, I usually don't season with anything else but pepper.

• Mix together 3 tablespoons of prepared horseradish and 16 ounces of sour cream. Add $1/2$ teaspoon salt and $1/2$ teaspoon white pepper. Stir well. Serve at room temperature with tenderloin and rolls, or warm as an accompaniment to roast prime rib. Try it, it's just the right touch.

# Essential Things
*Some trivia I thought I'd pass on since I'm between
sections and I don't know where else to put it.*

• These are the things I couldn't do without in my kitchen: My DLC-X Cuisinart, the Sunbeam mixer that we got 34 years ago as a wedding present — it's almost my "security blanket," a toaster-oven, a paring knife, a large and small chef's knife, and the extra-large cast-iron skillet I fry chicken in.

• The ingredients I feel "lost" without are: real butter — sweet and lightly salted — I buy Land o' Lakes, Durkees sauce, Tabasco sauce, fresh garlic, basil, and parsley.

• I love French's yellow mustard, Kraft Real mayonnaise, Heinz 57, Heinz ketchup, Kraft Cracker Barrel Coon cheese, Saga Blue cheese, and Peter Pan Extra-Chunky Peanut Butter — my staple "comfort" foods.

# Some Different Marinades
## For Grilled Chicken

• Mix 2 tablespoons of rosemary and basil with 1 cup of lemon juice and $1^1/_2$ cups oil — not olive. Chop 2 large pieces of fresh ginger and put everything in a blender and purée. Marinate the chicken in this for 2 to 3 hours. Grill or bake.

• Mix 1 cup olive oil with 10 chopped fresh sage leaves, 2 minced garlic cloves, 1 tablespoon balsamic vinegar, and $^1/_2$ cup lemon juice. Marinate the chicken in this for 2 hours and grill.

• Mix 2 tablespoons dried tarragon, 2 cloves minced garlic, 1 tablespoon ground ginger , 1 cup of oil, and $^2/_3$ cup lemon juice. Marinate the chicken in this for 2 hours and grill.

• *For Peggy's Fried Chicken, see page 36.*

• *For Aunt Callie's Buttermilk Fried Chicken, see page 37.*

• *For Chicken Salad Á La Rawls, see page 73.*

## An Easy Way To "Smoke" A Turkey

Put a 6- to 7-pound turkey breast in a ziplock bag. Mix together in a bowl: 4 bottles liquid smoke and $^1/_4$ cup packed brown sugar. Pour this over the turkey breast, and seal the bag, getting out most of the air. Place the bag in the refrigerator and let the turkey marinate for 2 days, turning the bag from side to side twice daily.

After 2 days, put the turkey breast side down in heavy-duty foil and pour the marinade in the cavity. Wrap tightly, and bake breast side down — you'll need to prop it up or put it on a V-shaped rack — in a 325-degree oven for 30 minutes a pound. It's really good!

• *How To Cook Turkey, see page 31.*

• *Turkey Tetrazzini, see page 80.*

# ~ Chicken Sauce For Spaghetti ~

### Aunt Callie's Chicken Spaghetti

This recipe is one that my Aunt Callie gave me a long time ago. As I have mentioned, Callie is a wonderful lady and cook — if you doubt me, just ask her!

| | |
|---|---|
| 2 onions, finely chopped | 1 large can of sliced |
| 1 cup finely chopped celery | mushrooms |
| 1 large green pepper, finely | 2 teaspoons chili powder |
| chopped | 3 cups reserved chicken broth |
| 3 tablespoons butter | salt and pepper to taste |
| 1 (4- to 5-pound) hen, boil, | grated sharp Cheddar or |
| chop meat, and reserve broth | Parmesan cheese |
| 2 cans of Ro-Tel tomatoes and | |
| green chiles, chopped | |

Sauté the onions, celery, and green pepper in the butter. Add the chopped chicken, tomatoes and green chiles, mushrooms, chili powder, and chicken broth. Simmer for 1 hour. Adjust seasonings, and serve over spaghetti or rice. Sprinkle either sharp Cheddar or Parmesan on top. Serves 10 to 12.

### Tipsy Chicken Spahetti

This one contains white wine and has an Italian flavor. It's my adaptation of the original recipe given to me by a friend, Ann Gayle Gupton Hall. She and her husband, Dwight, have been friends of ours for years!

| | |
|---|---|
| 2 cloves of garlic | 1 small can of sliced black olives |
| 1 tablespoon butter | 1 small jar of pimento-stuffed |
| 2 tablespoons olive oil | olives, sliced |
| 4 cups reserved chicken broth | 1 teaspoon oregano |
| 1 large can of tomato paste | 1 tablespoon dried parsley |
| 1 cup white wine such as Chablis | 8 ounces mild Cheddar cheese, |
| 1 (4- to 5-pound) hen, boil, | shredded |
| shred meat, and reserve broth | grated Parmesan cheese |

Sauté the garlic in the butter and oil and remove and discard it. Add the broth, tomato paste, white wine, shredded chicken, olives, and seasonings. Let cook for 1 hour. Add the Cheddar cheese and cook until all is blended. Serve over spaghetti; sprinkle with grated Parmesan. Serves 10 to 12.

# ❧ Steamed Mussels ❧

The first time I had mussels was in a small restaurant in Sausalito, across the Golden Gate Bridge from the city that has a piece of my heart, San Francisco. I really believe that I left the rest of it in Italy — except, of course, for the parts reserved for Buck and my family and friends!

First, rinse 1 bag of mussels (about 20 to 25) and remove the fuzzy beard. Discard any that have broken shells or remain open when rinsed. Set aside. Next, in a large skillet, sauté in 2 tablespoons olive oil: 1/4 cup finely minced shallots, 2 finely minced garlic cloves, and 1 tablespoon parsley. Add the juice of 1 lemon and a few grinds of pepper. Put 2 cups of white wine (I like to use Chardonnay here) in the skillet and turn the heat to high. Add the mussels, cover, and cook, covered, for 4 to 5 minutes. Remove the cover and discard any mussels that haven't opened. Immediately put the mussels in a bowl and spoon the sautéing broth over them. Enjoy! Serves 4.

# ❧ Scallops On The Grill ❧

Buy large sea scallops for this. Thread the scallops onto skewers with slices of bacon that you "snake" along between them. Brush the skewers with teriyaki sauce and grill, turning often so they don't burn.

# ❧ "Fake" Abalone ❧

Abalone is a very expensive shellfish. A chef in a San Francisco restaurant told me a way to "make" abalone. It wasn't until afterwards that I sort of wondered if this is what he served instead of the abalone we ordered!

In a glass dish, pour bottled clam juice over boneless chicken breasts, completely covering them. Place a piece of Saran over the bowl, and refrigerate for 24 hours, turning them over in the clam juice once or twice. Sauté in a small amount of butter and lemon juice. Sprinkle with a little pepper and fresh chives and parsley. Slice thinly and spoon some lemon butter sauce over the top.

## Notes ❧

• *For The Best Tuna Casserole, see page 79.*

• *Oysters–for the way I cook scalloped oysters and wild rice and oysters, see page 97.*

• *For Daddy's Poached Salmon, see page 20.*

• *For Peggy's Stuffed Red Snapper, see page 39.*

**Notes**

## ≫ Buck's Grilled Fresh Tuna Or Swordfish ≫

Marinate the fish in one of the following:

• $^1/_2$ cup white wine, 1 tablespoon Lea & Perrins Worcestershire sauce, 2 tablespoons lemon or lime juice, and 1 teaspoon Grey Poupon Dijon mustard.

• $^1/_2$ cup soy sauce, 1 teaspoon sesame oil, 2 teaspoons sesame seed, and 2 teaspoons mustard seed.

• Or spread both sides with Grey Poupon Dijon mustard and sprinkle with black pepper.

Grill just until the fish flakes easily.

## Fresh Grouper Or Flounder With Hazelnut And Artichoke ≫ Lemon Butter Sauce ≫

*My "try" at recreating a favorite dish from Billy's Tap Room in Ormond Beach, Florida. Buy 1 fish fillet per person. There is enough sauce to serve 4.*

Lightly dust the fish with flour and sauté in 2 tablespoons of oil over high heat. After both sides are quickly browned, remove the fish from the skillet and place on a baking sheet sprayed with Pam. Place in a preheated 375-degree oven and finish cooking about 10 minutes. While the fish is cooking, make the sauce.

### Hazelnut and Artichoke Lemon Butter Sauce

Melt $^1/_4$ cup butter in a skillet. Sauté 1 finely minced shallot. Add $^1/_2$ cup of toasted hazelnuts or pecans and sauté. Add 1 tablespoon drained capers and sauté. Put 1 can of drained, halved artichoke hearts in the pan. When they have sautéed for a few minutes, add a bit of fresh grind pepper — 2 or 3 turns.

Now to finish, add the juice of 1 lemon and heat on high just about 10 or 15 seconds. Take the fish from the oven and place on a plate.

Spoon the sauce over the fish and serve.

# Wild Things

I soak any game—from duck to venison—in my secret marinade to take away any "gamey" flavor.

My secret? ¹/₄ cup cider vinegar mixed with 1 bottle of Tabasco Bloody Mary Mix! My theory is that—if tomato juice removes skunk spray odor and most marinades contain the same seasonings in Bloody Mary mix, then why not use a mix! I like Tabasco Bloody Mary Mix the best, and I add the vinegar because that is what Peggy used to rub lamb with to remove any strong "mutton" flavors. This strange combination has always worked for me.

Just let the game soak for 8 to 12 hours or overnight, wipe the meat dry and brush with any cooking sauce or glaze you prefer. Some of the ones I use are listed below:

• If I am fixing duck, I brush it with a mixture of 1 tablespoon Lea & Perrins Worcestershire sauce, ¹/₂ cup honey, and 1 cup orange marmalade.

• When grilling venison, I brush the meat with a mixture of 1 tablespoon Lea & Perrins Worcestershire sauce and 1 stick of butter.

## ~☞ Venison Sausage ☜~
### *This a special treat to do with ground venison.*

For each pound of ground venison, you will need:

> 1 teaspoon anise seed
> 1 teaspoon Colman's dry mustard
> 1 teaspoon garlic powder
> 1 teaspoon liquid smoke
> 1 teaspoon pepper
> 1 teaspoon curing salt

Mix well and put in a bowl. Cover and refrigerate for 24 hours, remixing the meat 2 or 3 times. After 24 hours, roll the meat into a log shape and wrap it in cheesecloth. Bake it in a 250-degree oven for 3 or 4 hours. Cool.

Serve with assorted hot and sweet mustards and cocktail pumpernickel slices.

## Notes

*For Peggy's Southern Cornbread, see page 41.*

# ⪢ Aunt Callie's Sour Cream Cornbread ⪡
### *This is really almost a spoonbread, and man is it good!!*

| | |
|---|---|
| 1 small can of creamed corn | 4 ounces butter, melted |
| 8 ounces sour cream | 2 cups self-rising cornmeal |
| 2 eggs | $1/2$ cup self-rising flour |

Put all the ingredients in a mixing bowl and mix thoroughly. Put in an oblong dish that has been sprayed with Pam. Bake at 400 degrees for 30 to 40 minutes or until done.

*For Buck's White Bean Soup, see page 91.*

# ⪢ Hot Water Corn Cakes ⪡
### *Delicious puffs of crispy corn that are moist in the middle.*

Measure 2 cups of self-rising cornmeal into a bowl. Add enough boiling water to make a slightly damp mush — it should hold it's shape when spooned, but not be dry. Heat 2 cups oil in a skillet and fry heaping spoonfuls of the mush until golden brown. Serve with plenty of butter. These are the corncakes like Nero's Cactus Canyon used to serve — the ones that Buck loves with his special White Bean Soup.

# Corn Cakes Like a Famous
## ～ⓔ Nashville Steak House Serves ⓔ～

A waiter divulged the ingredients to me, but not the proportions. These suit my tastes, but you can vary them to suit yourself. Cook them like you would pancakes — silver-dollar-size. Be sure and have lots of butter handy!!

| | | | |
|---|---|---|---|
| 2 | cups buttermilk | 1 | cup self-rising flour |
| 2 | cups self-rising cornmeal | | |

You'll need a skillet or a griddle to cook them on. Lightly grease it during cooking as necessary.

## ～ⓔ Corn Light Bread ⓔ～
### *Just like the bread made by a famous*
### *Franklin, Tennessee market.*

| | | | |
|---|---|---|---|
| 3$^1/_2$ | cups self-rising cornmeal | $^1/_2$ | cup oil |
| 3 | cups buttermilk | $^3/_4$ | cup sugar |

Mix all ingredients well and pour into a well greased loaf pan. Bake at 350 degrees for 1 hour. Turn the oven off and let it sit in the oven for 1 hour. Turn it out of the pan. If you plan to serve it that day or the next, wrap in a damp cloth and put it in the refrigerator. If, however, you plan to serve it at a later date, wrap the cooled loaf in plastic wrap and then in foil and freeze.

## ❧ Notes

*The first time I ever had these was at the home of Blanche and "Curt" Curtis in Greenville, South Carolina. We lived in that wonderful town for three years—from August, 1976 to June, 1979. Buck was head of Volunteer Capital Corporation's Eastern Division, overseeing the building and operation of the Wendy's Old Fashioned Hamburger Restaurants in Volunteer's franchised territory East of the Mississippi River.*

*Volunteer Capital Corporation would later become Winners Corporation and be the largest Wendy's franchisee. Buck would later be promoted to president and CEO of Winners Corporation. Anyway, living in Greenville those three years was a very special time in our lives— we loved the city and South Carolina! Blanche and Curt lived across the street from us. They were, and still are, our friends.*

## ❧ Benne Seed Biscuits ❧

***Try these—they're quite unique. Oh, yes.
Benne seeds are unhulled sesame seeds.***

| | |
|---|---|
| 1 cup toasted benne seeds | ³/₄ cup shortening |
| 2 cups unsifted flour | ¹/₄ cup ice water (approximately) |
| 1 teaspoon salt | coarse salt |
| ¹/₄ to ¹/₂ teaspoon cayenne pepper | |

Toast the benne seeds in a 250-degree oven—watch closely! Mix the flour, salt, and cayenne pepper. Cut in the shortening. Mix in the toasted benne seeds. Add the ice water and mix well. The dough should be like pie crust dough. Roll out to ¹/₂-inch thickness and cut small rounds—I use a spice jar top. Place on a cookie sheet and bake at 300 degrees for 20 to 30 minutes. Sprinkle with coarse salt while they are still hot. Keep in a tin and reheat before serving.

## ❧ Anne's Dinner Rolls ❧

***Buck's mother, Anne, is world famous for her rolls—at the very least, she is famous for them in our family! Here is her recipe.***

Dissolve 2 yeast cakes in 1 cup of cold water. Add 2 eggs and beat well and set aside.

Beat together ¹/₂ cup shortening, ¹/₂ cup softened butter, ³/₄ cup sugar, 2 teaspoons salt, and 1 cup boiling water.

Beat in the yeast mixture. Add 6 cups of flour to this and beat. After mixing well, refrigerate for 12 hours. Roll out and cut. Let rise for 1¹/₂ to 2 hours before baking. Brush with melted butter and bake in a 375-degree oven until done and browned.

# ❧ Sutherland Christmas Nut Bread ❧

| | |
|---|---|
| 1 **tablespoon sugar** | 2 **tablespoons butter or** |
| 1 **cake yeast (1 envelope of dry** | **shortening** |
| **will work also)** | $^1/_3$ **cup sugar** |
| 1 **cup milk, scalded and cooled** | 1 **egg** |
| **to lukewarm** | $^1/_3$ **teaspoon salt** |
| 3 **cups flour** | $^3/_4$ **cup chopped pecans** |

Make the sponge by mixing the 1 tablespoon sugar with the yeast. Add to the lukewarm milk, and add 1$^1/_4$ cups of the flour. Beat this thoroughly and set aside to rise for 50 minutes.

Cream the butter and add the $^1/_3$ cup sugar and the egg—beat well and add to the sponge mixture. Beat and add the rest of the flour and the salt. Knead this well. Add the nuts and knead again slightly to mix in the nuts. Place the dough in a lightly greased bowl and set in a warm place to rise for 50 to 60 minutes or until doubled. After rising, shape into a loaf, place in a greased large loaf pan, and let rise another hour. Bake in a 350-degree oven for 45 minutes.

# ❧ How Did She Do That? ❧

### *An unusual way to bake and to serve bread.*

Defrost 1 package of Rich's Roll Dough. Dip each piece in 1 stick of melted butter and layer in an angel food cake pan. Bake in a 350-degree oven for 20 to 25 minutes. Turn out when cooled. It will look like a pull-apart loaf of bread with a hole in the middle.

To serve: Pull the bread apart—very gently. Place a tall balloon wine glass in the center "hole" and put the bread back together. Put butter curls in the wine glass—it's a show stopper!

*This is another special recipe from our dear friends, Patricia and Pete Sutherland. Patricia makes it every Christmas. She, like me, "doesn't bake much," and when she does, it is for a holiday or special occasion. This is really wonderful toasted for sandwiches and I bet it would make delicious French toast! This is a very old recipe.*

## Notes

• *For Peggy's "know how" on veggies, see pages 31 to 34.*

• *For Peggy's squash and squash casserole, see page 32.*

## Onion-Stuffed Mushrooms

I slice an onion very thin and cook it in a skillet with a little olive oil until it is golden. I add 1 mashed clove of garlic and cook for a minute. Then I add 1 teaspoon of dried basil and toss. Pile this in fresh mushroom caps. Bake in a 375-degree oven until the mushrooms are done. You could do this with portabella mushrooms also.

## A Different Squash Dish

Slice 6 large summer squash and put in a pot with 1 sliced onion. Cook, covered, in a small amount of water. When soft, drain and put in a greased baking dish. Melt a stick of butter and add ½ cup of packed brown sugar to it. Crumble Ritz crackers over the squash and evenly pour the butter mixture over all. Bake in a 375-degree oven for 20 to 30 minutes until it is bubbly and the top is browned.

## Caramel Carrots

Cook 6 sliced carrots in water until done. Combine with a mixture of ½ cup of packed brown sugar — that you have cooked until it is syrupy, 1 tablespoon butter, and ½ teaspoon orange peel.

## Brown Butter Sauce For Vegetables

• Cook 1 stick of butter until it is light brown. Pour the butter over hot steamed green beans, asparagus, or broccoli.

• Add pecans, walnuts, or almonds to the butter and sauté them while the butter is browning. Pour this over vegetables, over chicken breasts or fish...Delicious!

# ❧ Easy Vegetable Soufflés ☙
### *Make any vegetable into a soufflé.*

Purée the vegetable after steaming. Add ½ cup heavy cream and 2 eggs for every 2 cups of purée. Bake in a greased dish in a 400-degree oven until puffed and set.

# ❧ Potatoes ☙

### Potatoes On The Grill
Slice 4 potatoes and 2 onions. Layer on a sheet of heavy-duty foil, dot with butter, and sprinkle with salt, pepper, thyme, rosemary, and parsley. Seal the foil and place on the grill. Cook for about 30 to 40 minutes or until tender.

### Scalloped Potatoes Jarvis
One of Buck's oldest and dearest friends is Peter Jarvis. Peter and Buck were in the same class at Father Ryan High School. Peter and his wife, Cindy, live in Minneapolis. We try to see them as often as our busy schedules permit. Peter's mother and father, Gabrielle and Clayton Jarvis, were lovely people. Buck and I would visit with them often and enjoyed them as much as we did Peter. Gabrielle was an excellent cook and this is how she made scalloped potatoes.

Layer in a buttered casserole dish: thinly sliced potatoes and thinly sliced onions, starting and ending with a layer of potatoes. Dot every other layer with butter and sprinkle with salt and pepper. Pour milk — or half-and-half — over the layers to just cover the top layer. Place in a 325-degree oven and bake for 1½ hours. You may need to cover the top with foil if it begins to get too brown.

*You can substitute almost any vegetable for the potatoes — squash, eggplant, tomatoes, etc.*

*• For Peggy's potatoes — baked, stuffed, or mashed, see page 34.*

*• For Peggy's sweet potatoes and marshmallow sweet potatoes, see page 34.*

*• For Au Gratin Potatoes, see page 30.*

*• For Peggy's Fried Corn, see page 31.*

*• For Ene's Fried Corn, see page 31.*

*• For Grandmother's creamed corn, see page 25.*

*• For Escalloped Corn, see page 80.*

## Notes

## ⤞ Gourmet Gala ⤟

***Believe it or not, the following is the recipe that won us the 1985
Gourmet Gala top prize—the Corning Creative Cookery Award!***

They asked for five recipes—one in each of five categories: appetizer, soup, entrée, vegetable, and dessert. I submitted these:

> Stuffed Red Onions with Mornay Sauce
> Gravlax with Mustard Dill Sauce
> Charleston and Greenville Crab Bisque
> Bluefish Southampton
> Crunchy Country Pie

*The one they chose was the onion—only, they didn't know that
I had made it up as I was writing the recipe!! I had never fixed
it and I wasn't even sure that it would work!*

The only thing to do was start cooking! I bought every red onion in Brentwood and every package of frozen spinach. I'm sure I made the recipe a million times—well, at least 100 times. Anyway, after I had the recipe perfected—it had to be the exact one I had submitted—no changes or they might guess what I had done, the next step was coming up with a novel presentation.

What can be done to make a stuffed onion appealing? I decided to cut petals out of the outer two layers so that when it cooked they would fan out and look like petals. Then, I decided to put a dab of red caviar on top of the dollop of Mornay Sauce that was put on the top of the onion "flower."

As a final garnish, I made "fans" out of green onions, and inserted a purple chrysanthemum in the center, making a flower that we would place on each judge's plate as we served them.

With that done, I thought it would be fun to have at our booth an assortment of edible things that I had made using the onion's spinach stuffing. This would be a way to possibly impress the judges—Nathalie Dupree and Craig Claiborne were to be two of them. I created a spinach wheat cracker, a spinach gnocchi, a cold terrine of onion and spinach layers, and a sausage/spinach pâté. All of these things were made with the spinach stuffing as the main ingredient!! We served a lovely sparkling wine from California—Schramsburg Blanc de Noir. We even impressed ourselves!!

# Stuffed Red Onions
## ~ With Mornay Sauce ~

6  medium red onions
1  bunch parsley
4  celery ribs
1  bunch green onions (tops only)
1  (10-ounce) package frozen chopped spinach
1/4  cup sweet butter
1/4  cup reserved bacon drippings

2  ablespoons Lea & Perrins Worcestershire sauce
1  teaspoon Tabasco sauce
salt to taste
1/2  cup plain bread crumbs
2  eggs
1/2  cup heavy cream
8  slices bacon, crisp-fried and crumbled (reserve drippings)

Cut the tops from the onions, and a small slice from the root end if needed to make it sit up straight. Scoop out the centers, leaving 2 layers on the sides and not going through the bottom. Reserve one of the centers and save or freeze the others for use at another time. Cut the outer layer of the onion into pointed petals, wrap them in foil and refrigerate until ready to stuff. Combine the reserved onion center, the parsley, celery, and green onion tops in the food processor and chop very finely. Thaw the spinach; squeeze the moisture out. Melt the butter and the bacon drippings in a large skillet. Add the chopped vegetables and cook over low heat for 10 or 15 minutes. Add the spinach, seasonings, and bread crumbs; stir well. Remove from the heat. Beat the eggs with the cream and stir into the spinach mixture. Add the crumbled bacon and mix well. Stuff into the onions and place them in a buttered baking dish. Bake at 350 degrees for 45 minutes. When cooked, if they aren't already down, gently pull the petals down to resemble flower petals. Serve with a dollop of Mornay Sauce on top. Serves 6.

## Mornay Sauce:

1/4 cup sweet butter
1/4 cup flour
1/2 cup heavy cream
1 1/2 cups milk

1/2 cup freshly grated Parmesan cheese
1/2 teaspoon salt
1/4 teaspoon white pepper

Melt the butter and stir in the flour. Whisk for 2 minutes—do not let it get brown. Add the cream and milk, whisking constantly. Add the cheese and the salt and white pepper. Cook for 3 to 5 minutes or until thick and smooth, stirring constantly.

## ✐ Notes

*Here are the other recipes I submitted. I still think any other of them would have been a tastier choice!*

## ⤞ Gravlax with Mustard Dill Sauce ⤝

| | |
|---|---|
| 3 tablespoons coarse salt | 2 thoroughly boned salmon |
| 1 tablespoon sugar | fillets (1½ pounds each) |
| 2 tablespoons coarsely ground pepper | 2 bunches fresh dill |

Mix salt, sugar, and pepper. Rub half the mixture on the flesh side of each salmon fillet. Lay 1 fillet skin-side down in a deep glass dish. Lay dill on fillet. Place other fillet skin-side up on top if fillet with dill. Tie the fillets together with twine. Cover with plastic wrap and place a heavy weight (at least 5 pounds) on top of the fillets. I use a board or bricks. Place dish in the refrigerator for 3 days, turning the fillets twice a day. After 3 days, remove fillets from dish, untie them, and discard dill. Scrape off as much of the seasoning mixture as possible. Serve right away or they will keep refrigerated for up to 2 weeks.

To serve: Pat fish dry and slice thinly on the diagonal. Serve with "party pumpernickle" and Mustard Dill Sauce. Serves 8 to 10.

### Mustard Dill Sauce

| | |
|---|---|
| ¾ cup sugar | 1 (8-ounce) jar prepared |
| ½ cup water | mustard |
| 2 to 3 tablespoons dried dillweed | |

Heat sugar and water over medium heat until a thin syrup forms. Remove from heat and add dillweed; stir well. Add mustard; stir well. Let cool. Store in the refrigerator. Serve with Gravlax and as a sauce for other cold seafood such as shrimp, crab meat, or poached fish.

# Charleston and Greenville
## ~ Crab Bisque ~

1 generous pound white crab meat (if fresh is not available, use three 6-ounce cans white crab meat)

$^1/_4$ cup butter

1 small onion (purée in processor or blender)

2 tablespoons flour

2 cups milk

$^1/_2$ teaspoon Worchestershire sauce

$^1/_8$ to $^1/_4$ teaspoon Tabasco sauce

$^1/_4$ teaspoon powdered mace

salt to taste (be sure to taste first—because of the salt already in the butter, the Worcestershire, and Tabasco sauce, none may be needed)

2 cups heavy cream

$^1/_4$ cup sherry

Wash crab meat and drain well. Melt butter over low heat and add onion. Sauté a few minutes. Add flour; cook until well blended. Whisk in the milk, making sure there are no flour lumps. Add Worcestershire sauce, Tabasco sauce, mace, and salt (if needed). Stir well. Add crab meat. Transfer to a double boiler. Stir in heavy cream. Cook over low heat until well thickened (about 20 minutes), stirring occasionally. Add sherry; stir well. Take off heat and let sit, covered, for 10 to 15 minutes. Serve with chopped parsley sprinkled on top. Serves 6 to 8.

*This soup can be made with 1 pound chopped cooked shrimp.*

# ⤠ Bluefish Southampton ⤟

3 or 4 large onions, sliced ¼ inch thick and separated into rings
1 to 1½ sticks butter
salt and seasoned pepper to taste

5 pounds skinned bluefish
2 or 3 lemons, quartered and seeded
white wine

In a well-buttered deep pan, arrange onions so that you have a layer ½ inch thick. Dot well with butter. Layer bluefish over onions. Squeeze lemons over fish and put squeezed quarters around the fish. Sprinkle with salt and seasoned pepper. Pour wine in the pan to just the level of the onions — ½ inch. Cover tightly with foil. Place in a 400-degree oven and cook until fish flakes, about 25 to 30 minutes. Do not let all liquid evaporate. Remove from oven and let sit for 10 to 15 minutes, tightly covered. Serve each portion with some onions and sauce. Serves 8.

# ⤠ Crunchy Country Pie ⤟

1 stick butter
¼ cup flour
1 cup packed light brown sugar
2 eggs and 2 egg whites
1 teaspoon vanilla extract

1 cup chopped pecans or walnuts
6 ounces chocolate chips
1 pie shell

Melt butter over low heat. Remove from heat. Mix flour and brown sugar. Put whole eggs in blender and blend until frothy. Add to flour and brown sugar; stir well. Add vanilla, nuts, and chocolate chips; stir well. Whip egg whites until almost stiff. Fold into batter. Add cooled melted butter; stir well. Pour into pie shell. Bake at 275 degrees for 1 hour or until set. Serve warm or at room temperature.

# Triple Chocolate
## ⋙ Coconut Pecan Cake ⋘
### *This is my youngest son's favorite.*

1 small box Jell-O instant coconut or vanilla pudding mix

2 containers coconut pecan ready-to-spread frosting

1 box Duncan Hines chocolate cake mix

1 large box Jell-O instant chocolate pudding mix

4 eggs

1 cup water

1 stick butter, melted

$^1/_4$ cup oil

1 (12-ounce) bag chocolate chips (either Nestlé or Hershey's)

First, mix the small box of pudding with one of the containers of frosting and set aside. Mix the cake mix with the chocolate pudding mix, the eggs, the water, the butter, and the oil; mix thoroughly. Add the chocolate chips and mix well. Pour into a well greased and floured bundt pan. Now, spoon the reserved frosting-pudding mixture to make a circle on top the batter—don't let the frosting mixture touch the side of the pan. Bake at 350 degrees for 45 to 60 minutes. Let cool before turning out. Frost with the remaining container of frosting.

## ⋙ More Cake Flavors ⋘
### *Mix and bake as above.*

### White Chocolate
White cake mix, 4 egg whites, $^3/_4$ cup oil, 1 large box vanilla instant pudding mix, 2 teaspoons butter flavoring, 1 cup water, and 12 ounces white chocolate chips.

### Butterscotch
Yellow cake mix, 4 eggs, 1 stick melted butter, $^1/_4$ cup oil, 1 large box of either butterscotch or vanilla instant pudding mix, 1 cup water, and 12 ounces butterscotch chips.

### Orange or Lemon
Yellow cake mix, $^3/_4$ cup oil, 4 eggs, 1 large or 2 small boxes of orange or lemon Jell-O gelatin mix, 1 cup water, 1 tablespoon dried orange or lemon peel, and 1 teaspoon orange or lemon flavoring.

*Peggy's Cakes and Frostings*

• *For Georgia Chocolate Cake, see page 42.*

• *For Orange Juice Coffee Cake, see page 44.*

• *For a true "pound" cake see page 43.*

• *For Mana's Tennessee Fruitcake, see page 23.*

*Make your favorite flavor cake just plain or add your choice of frosting and/or "tunnel."*

**✑ Notes**

# ❧ Carol Ann Pryor's Whipped Cream Cake ❧

*A special recipe from a dear friend.*
*This is my oldest son's favorite.*

4   eggs, beat until light yellow
   and thick
1   cup sugar (beat with the eggs
   after they have been beaten)

1   cup flour (sift with 1
   teaspoon baking powder, and
   mix with the eggs)
1   teaspoon vanilla extract
   (mix into the batter)

Mix as directed, and pour evenly into three 8-inch greased and floured cake pans. Bake at 350 degrees for 25 to 30 minutes. Turn out, let cool, and frost with the following:

3   cups heavy cream
1   cup sugar

1   teaspoon vanilla extract

Whip the cream with the sugar and vanilla. When you frost the cake, put fresh strawberries or toasted walnut halves on the top and sides of the cake. Keep the cake in the refrigerator.

# Triple Chocolate
# ❧ Pudding-In-The-Middle Cake ❧

*This is my middle son's favorite.*

2   large boxes Jell-O instant
   chocolate pudding mix
milk
1   box Duncan Hines Butter
   Recipe chocolate cake mix
4   eggs

1   cup water
1   stick butter, melted
¼   cup oil
1   (12-ounce) bag chocolate
   chips (either Nestlé or
   Hershey's)

First, mix 1 box of pudding using ½ the amount of milk called for and set aside. In a large bowl, mix the cake mix with the eggs, water, butter, oil, and the other box of pudding. After thoroughly mixing, add the chocolate chips. Pour the cake into a well greased and floured bundt pan. Now, carefully spoon the reserved pudding to make a circle on top the batter — don't let the pudding touch the side of the pan. Bake for 45 to 60 minutes in a 350-degree oven. Let cool completely before inverting. Sprinkle with powdered sugar.

# ≈ California Date Cake ≈

| | |
|---|---|
| 1 cup of cake flour | 4 eggs, well beaten |
| 2 teaspoons baking powder | 1 teaspoon vanilla extract |
| 1/8 pound butter (it's 2 ounces) | 1 pound pitted dates, chopped |
| 1 cup sugar | 1 pound chopped Brazil nuts |

Sift the flour and baking powder and mix with the creamed butter and sugar, beaten eggs, and everything else. Put in a shallow greased and floured cake pan. Bake at 325 degrees for 1 hour. During the baking, pat the cake down so that it won't rise too much—it makes a richer cake.

# ≈ A Simple Upside-Down Cake ≈

Prepare a small box of white or yellow cake mix—I use Jiffy brand.

Melt in an ovenproof skillet: 1/4 cup butter: then, add 1/2 cup packed brown sugar and the juice from a small can of sliced pineapple. Cook this until it is syrupy. Take the skillet from the heat, lay the pineapple slices in the syrup, put a maraschino cherry in the center of each pineapple slice, and place pecan halves top side down around the pineapple.

Pour the cake mix over this and put in a 350-degree oven. Bake for 40 or 50 minutes until done. Let cool slightly before inverting onto a platter. Serve with a dollop of whipped cream.

*This a recipe that was given to Mana by her "Cousin Frances" Drake on trips to California. "Cousin Frances" was married to Mana's cousin, "Cousin Gene" Drake, and they lived in Santa Monica. "Cousin Gene" used to say she was a "dandy good cook"!*

**Notes**

# ~ A Few Of Aunt Mamie's Cakes ~

Aunt Mamie was Buck's great-great-aunt. She was Buck's mother, Anne's great-aunt. She was Anne's mother, Ene's aunt. That makes her Ene's mother's sister—Whew!! She was born in Texas and moved to Nashville about 1900 after her husband, who was also her first cousin, was killed in a railroad accident. She was the dietician for the Tennessee State Penitentiary for many years. She was very successful—she was able to buy three homes and owned all of them at the same time!! The houses were on Acklen Avenue, here in Nashville. Mamie, Ene, Ene's sister Mae, Anne, and Anne's sister Dot all lived together. I never had the pleasure of meeting Mamie, but from all I've heard, she was quite ahead of her time.

These recipes are in her personal cooking journal. Some were typed and some were written. I've chosen a few to include in my "journal" of Southern Cooking.

- *Father's Spice Cake*

- *Mother's Fruitcake*

- *Jam Cake Fine*

- *White Fruitcake*

- *Swans Down Angel Food Cake*

## Father's Spice Cake

*I assume this was Mamie's father's recipe.*

| | |
|---|---|
| 1/2 cup shortening | 1/4 teaspoon salt |
| 1 1/2 cups packed brown sugar | 1/2 teaspoon each baking |
| 2 eggs | powder, baking soda, cloves, |
| 3/4 cup sour milk (use | and allspice |
| buttermilk) | 1 teaspoon each mace, |
| 1/4 cup molasses | cinnamon, ginger, and nutmeg |
| 2 cups flour | Raisin Filling |

Cream the shortening and brown sugar. Add eggs, beating after each one. Stir in the sour milk and molasses. Sift the rest of the ingredients together and fold into the first mixture. Put in 2 or 3 greased and floured cake pans. Bake at 375 degrees for 25 minutes. When cool, put Raisin Filling between the layers and on top of the cake.

### Raisin Filling

1/4 cup soft butter, 1 cup powdered sugar, 1/4 teaspoon lemon extract, and 3/4 cup raisins. Mix all together.

## Mother's Fruitcake

Makes a 24-pound fruitcake!!

1½ pounds soft butter
2 pounds brown sugar
20 eggs, separated (and yolks and whites beaten)
1 tablespoon ground cloves
4 pounds raisins and currants (dust with flour)
2 pounds each dates and figs (cut and dust with flour)
1 pound each crystallized cherries and pineapple (cut and dust with flour)

½ pound citron (cut and dust with flour)
2 pounds flour
1 (6-ounce) glass grape juice
1 small bottle vanilla extract
grated peel from ½ pound oranges and lemons

Cream the butter and brown sugar. Add the beaten egg yolks and cloves and fold in the beaten egg whites. Starting with a handful of fruit, add the fruit and flour alternately, a bit at a time, until all is incorporated. Add the grape juice, vanilla, and orange and lemon peel. Put in a greased and floured large, deep, round pan. Bake in a 250-degree oven for 2 to 3 hours.

## Jam Cake Fine

1½ cups sugar
⅔ cup soft butter
3 eggs
1 teaspoon baking soda
1 cup buttermilk
3½ cups flour

1 cup of jam (any kind)
1 tablespoon cocoa
1 teaspoon each cinnamon and allspice
2 cups raisins (optional)

Cream sugar and butter. Add eggs and beat. Add baking soda to the buttermilk and stir in. Add the rest of the ingredients and mix well. Pour into 2 greased and floured cake pans. Bake at 375 degrees for 25 or 30 minutes.

Frost with the following icing:

Mix 1½ cups sour cream and 2 cups sugar and cook in a double boiler until thick. Cool slightly and beat in 1 tablespoon soft butter and 1 teaspoon vanilla extract. Add ½ cup chopped pecans. Spread on the cake.

*Again, I assume this was Mamie's mother's recipe.*

**Notes**

## White Fruitcake

| | |
|---|---|
| 1  pound soft butter | 1/2 pound each citron and raisins |
| 3 1/3 cups flour | (dredge in 2/3 cup flour) |
| 2  cups white sugar | 2  pounds blanched and split |
| 12 egg whites, stiffly beaten (and | almonds |
| divided in half) | |

Cream the butter and beat with the 3 1/3 cups flour. Beat the sugar with half the egg whites until very light. Mix the floured fruits and almonds with the butter mixture. Mix the sugar mixture in. Lastly, fold in the remaining egg whites. Put in a greased and floured large, deep, round pan. Bake at 250 degrees for 2 hours.

## Swans Down Angel Food Cake

*This is Ene's "mile high" cake.*

| | |
|---|---|
| 1  cup Swans Down cake flour | 1 1/4 cups sifted granulated sugar |
| 1  cup egg whites | 3/4 teaspoon vanilla extract |
| 1/4 teaspoon salt | 1/4 teaspoon almond extract |
| 1  teaspoon cream of tartar | |

Sift the flour one time and spoon into a measuring cup to the 1-cup mark. Sift again 4 more times. Beat the egg whites with the salt until foamy. Add the cream of tartar and continue beating until they are stiff to peak, but not dry. Add the sugar 2 tablespoons at a time and fold in carefully until all the sugar is used. Fold the flavorings in. Sift the flour a little at a time and gently fold in until all is used. Put in an ungreased angel food cake pan and cut through the batter 4 or 5 times with a spatula and rap 1 or 2 times on a table or counter to remove any large air bubbles. Put in a cool oven and turn the temperature to 275 degrees. After 30 minutes, increase the oven temperature to 325 degrees and bake for 30 more minutes. Remove the cake from the oven and invert the pan at least 1 hour before taking the cake out of the pan.

# Felice's California
## ✬ Cottage Cheese Torte ✬

### *This was a recipe she gave to Mana.*

## The Crust:

1 package Zwieback toast, crushed fine and mixed with 1 cup sugar, 1/2 cup melted butter, and 1 teaspoon cinnamon. Reserve 1/4 cup. Press the remaining crust in the bottom and up the side of a well greased springform pan.

## The Filling:

| | |
|---|---|
| 4 **eggs** | 1 **teaspoon vanilla extract** |
| 1 **cup sugar** | 8 **ounces cream** |
| 1/8 **teaspoon salt** | 1 1/2 **pounds cottage cheese** |
| **juice and zest of** 1/2 **lemon** | 1/4 **cup flour** |

Beat the eggs with the sugar until light and fluffy. Add the salt, the lemon juice and zest, vanilla, and the cream. Beat this well, then add the cheese and flour. Beat this well and push through a sieve to smooth out (I would put all of this in the processor and process until smooth).

Mix well and pour the mixture into the prepared springform pan. Sprinkle with the reserved crust. Bake in a 325-degree oven for 1 hour. Turn the oven off and let the torte sit in it for 1 hour. Serve cold.

You may add 1/2 cup chopped currants to the batter if desired.

*Felice was (are you ready?) Felice Jefferson Thomas Englebrecht Tefft. She was married to Cousin Frances' nephew, Nugent Thomas — at least "Nuge" was her first husband. That made her really no relation to Mana; but, because "Cousin Frances" was married to "Cousin Gene" and he was really Mana's cousin, it made "Nuge" and Felice kissin' kin.*

*So, Mana, Momma, and Ann saw them every time they were out in California. Felice and "Nuge" later divorced and "Nuge" married Else and they lived in Carmel, where Else still lives. Getting back to Felice, she wasn't pretty, but she had a wonderful sense of humor and was fun to be around and Mana, Momma, and Ann loved seeing her.*

## Notes

*The very first cheesecake I ever tasted was at Leb's Delicatessen in Atlanta. It was Strawberry Cheesecake and I thought it was the best thing that these then-12-year-old taste buds had ever tasted. Cheesecake is invariably my first choice when ordering dessert. I prefer plain with only a fruit topping. I have learned that there really isn't much that can be better than a wonderfully creamy, light— yet dense— plain cheesecake.*

*The same holds true for other things, too. If you want to know it it's a good pizza place, order "plain" cheese. If you want to know if an Italian restaurant is any good, order "plain" Alfredo sauce, or a simple tomato basil sauce. If the simplest is good then the rest will be good.*

*In a "meat and three" order mashed potatoes. If you can get a "plain" burger that's good, I'll be willing to bet that everything else is good. Nobody asked, but I love McCabe Pub's burgers!*

## ❧ A Couple Of Cheesecakes ❧

**The best cheesecake I ever had was at Wolf's Deli in New York City in 1984. I still haven't had any better! However, I do have one or two that are pretty darn good—so, here goes.**

### "Plain" Cheesecake

Cream together:

| | |
|---|---|
| 4 pounds softened Philadelphia cream cheese | 7 eggs, beating after each addition |
| 2¹/₂ cups sugar | 1 teaspoon each vanilla extract and lemon rind |

Pour this into a piecrust-lined 10-inch springform pan. Bake for 1¹/₂ hours in a water bath in a 325-degree oven. When done, remove from the water bath. Let cool completely before refrigerating. Serve cold with fruit or plain.

To make a water bath: Place the springform pan in a larger deep-sided pan and pour hot water in the larger pan to about halfway up the springform pan. Carefully put this in the oven.

*If you really want to know if the chef can make a good cheesecake, order "plain."*

## Three-Cheese Cheesecake

For the graham cracker crust:

Mix together: 1¼ cups graham cracker crumbs, ¼ cup sugar, and 3 tablespoons soft butter. Press in the bottom and up the side of the springform pan or pie pan.

For the cheesecake:

| | |
|---|---|
| **8 ounces each heavy cream, sour cream, ricotta cheese, and mascarpone cheese** | **1 cup sugar** |
| **32 ounces Philadelphia cream cheese** | **1 teaspoon each orange extract and lemon extract** |
| | **2 teaspoons vanilla extract** |
| | **4 eggs (beat after each addition)** |

Have all the ingredients at room temperature. Combine all but the eggs in a food processor until very creamy. Scrape down the sides and add the eggs, pulsing after each addition. Pour into the prepared springform pan and place in a 400-degree oven and bake for 5 minutes. Reduce the oven temperature to 300 degrees. Bake for approximately 1¼ hours. Let cool completely before refrigerating. Serve cold with fruit or plain.

*This one I usually bake in no crust, but a graham cracker crust would be fine — or a plain pastry crust.*

## Notes

### Peggy's Pies

• For Apple Pie, see page 45.

• For Pecan Pie, see page 46.

• For Southern Chess Pie, see page 46. (Chocolate and Coconut Chess Pie, too)

# Richland Country Club's
## Fabulous Famous Fudge Pie

### If you serve it just slightly warm—
### you'll swear you are in heaven!!

| | |
|---|---|
| 2 squares unsweet baking chocolate | 1/4 cup flour |
| 1 stick butter | 1 teaspoon vanilla extract |
| 1 cup sugar | 1 cup pecans |
| 2 eggs | 1 unbaked pie shell |

Melt the chocolate with the butter and let cool. Add the rest of the ingredients; mix well. Pour into an unbaked pie shell. Bake at 275 degrees for 45 to 55 minutes. Incredible!!

## My Version Of Richland's Country Pie
### Delicious!!

| | |
|---|---|
| 2 egg whites | 1 teaspoon vanilla extract |
| 1 stick butter, melted and cooled | 1/4 cup flour |
| 1 1/2 cups packed light brown sugar | 6 ounces chocolate chips |
| 2 eggs | 1/2 cup each slivered almonds, hazelnuts, and pecans |
| | 1 unbaked pie shell |

Beat the egg whites stiff. Mix the butter, brown sugar, eggs, vanilla, flour, and chocolate chips and fold in the egg whites. Fold in the nuts. Put in an unbaked pie shell. Bake at 350 degrees for 30 to 45 minutes.

# ❧ Aunt Mamie's Coconut Custard Pie ❧

3 eggs, separate 2 of the eggs
and beat the 2 egg whites stiff
2 cups milk
$1/2$ cup sugar

$1/2$ teaspoon vanilla extract
$1/8$ teaspoon salt
1 can Baker's coconut
1 prebaked pie shell

Beat the 2 egg yolks and the whole egg until creamy, add the milk, $1/2$ cup sugar, vanilla, salt, and half the can of coconut. Put in a prebaked pie shell. Bake in a 350-degree oven for 25 minutes. Remove from the oven and let cool. When cool, spread with the meringue and sprinkle with the rest of the coconut. Put back in the oven at 350 degrees and bake for 10 minutes to brown the meringue.

# ❧ Aunt Mamie's Bridge Butterscotch Pie ❧

$1^1/2$ cups sugar
$1/4$ cup water
4 cups milk
2 tablespoons butter
$1/8$ teaspoon salt

3 eggs, well beaten
$1/2$ cup cornstarch
1 teaspoon vanilla extract
1 prebaked pie shell

First put $1/2$ cup of the sugar and the $1/4$ cup of water in a saucepan and boil until it is a golden brown. In a double boiler, heat the milk, the 1 cup sugar, the butter, and salt. When warm, add the caramelized sugar; stir well. Beat the eggs, add the cornstarch, and temper by adding a small amount of the milk mixture. Then add this to the hot milk and cook and stir until thick. Add the vanilla and pour into a prebaked pie shell. Cool and serve with whipped cream.

**Notes**

## ❧ Aunt Mamie's Sunshine Lemon Pie ☙

4 eggs, separated, and the
   whites beaten stiff
¹/₂ cup sugar
the juice and rind (zest) of 1
   lemon

1 envelope gelatin, dissolved in
   ¹/₃ cup water
1 prebaked pie shell

Put the egg yolks, the sugar, and the lemon juice and rind in a double boiler. Cook, stirring constantly, until thick and creamy. Remove from the heat and add the dissolved gelatin. Cool. Fold in the stiff egg whites and put in a prebaked pie shell. Chill and serve with whipped cream.

## ❧ Mae's Lemon Pie ☙

Mae was Mae Montgomery — Buck's great-aunt, his mother, Anne's aunt, and his grandmother Ene's sister — she was one of the 3 women who were able to, in a time where it wasn't fashionable, be successful in a world dominated by men. She was a buyer for women's ready-to-wear for Castner- Knott in the 1940s and 1950s. She was a true "business woman," and loved what she did. This is her lemon pie — she was nicknamed the "lemon drop kid" by family and friends because she added "just a touch of lemon" to almost everything she made.

1 tablespoon butter
1 cup hot water
1 cup sugar
3 tablespoons cornstarch
3 beaten egg yolks

the juice and peel of 1 lemon
1 baked pie shell
3 egg whites
3 tablespoons sugar
1 teaspoon vanilla extract

Melt butter in hot water. Add 1 cup sugar and 3 tablespoons cornstarch and cook over medium heat until thick. Add the 3 beaten egg yolks; stir for 3 minutes. Then, add the lemon juice and the peel. Pour into a baked pie shell. Cover with meringue, made by whipping 3 egg whites with 3 tablespoons sugar and 1 teaspoon vanilla.

# ᴈ Dad's Favorite Buttermilk Pie ᴈ

*Dad was William Hussung, Iva's husband, Big Buck's father,
and Buck's grandfather.*

½ cup butter
2 tablespoons flour
1 cup sugar
3 egg yolks
1 cup buttermilk
½ teaspoon nutmeg

1 teaspoon cinnamon
1 cup raisins
1 baked pie shell
3 egg whites
3 tablespoons sugar

Melt the butter in a saucepan. Add the flour and cook for 2 minutes. Add the 1 cup sugar, egg yolks, buttermilk, nutmeg, and cinnamon. Cook for 4 or 5 minutes or until thickened, stirring constantly. Lastly, stir in the raisins and pour into a baked pie shell.

Beat the egg whites until foamy. Add the 3 tablespoons sugar gradually, while beating, and continue beating until stiff peaks form. Spread over the filling, sealing to the crust. Brown the meringue-topped pie in a 350-degree oven.

# ᴈ Date Macaroon Pie ᴈ

12 saltines, crushed and
    rolled fine
1 cup sugar
12 dates, chopped

1½ cups pecans, chopped
1 teaspoon each baking powder
    and almond extract
3 egg whites, stiffly beaten

Fold all the ingredients into the beaten egg whites. Put in a greased pie pan. Bake at 350 degrees for 30 minutes. Serve with ice cream. Yum.

*Iva Hussung was Buck's grandmother, and Big Buck's mother. She was an only child, was raised by her grand-mother, and married Big Buck's father when she was very young. They were the parents of six children and lived in Sterling, Illinois, all their lives. She was a really good cook—Buck remembers lots and lots of good food at "Grandma's" house when he visited.*

• *This is a Bertolli Bakes Better Contest Prize Winner.*

• *Make Chocolate Hazelnut Pie, a variation of Almond Pie. Omit the almond oil, the almond extract, and the sliced almonds, and add ¼ cup unsweetened cocoa, ½ cup chopped hazelnuts, and increase the vanilla from 1 teaspoon to 1 tablespoon, and increase the Bertolli Light olive oil from ½ cup to ¾ cup.*

# ꙅ Iva's Angel Food Pie ꙥ

*This is a pie that everybody loved—it's an unusual one, too.*

| | |
|---|---|
| 2  tablespoons cornstarch | 1  baked pie shell |
| ¼ cup cold water | 1  cup heavy cream, whipped |
| 1  cup sugar |    with 1 teaspoon vanilla |
| 1¼ cups boiling water |    extract and 2 tablespoons |
| 1  teaspoon vanilla extract |    sugar |
| 2  egg whites, stiffly beaten | |

Dissolve the cornstarch in the ¼ cup cold water. Add this and the sugar to the 1¼ cups boiling water. Cook until thick, stirring constantly, and remove from the heat. Add the vanilla and pour the cooked mixture over the stiffly beaten egg whites while beating constantly. Put in a baked pie shell.

Put in the refrigerator to chill. Put the whipped cream on top and serve chilled.

# ꙅ Almond Pie ꙥ

I created this pie using one of my old family recipes for a traditional Southern dessert called Chess Pie. The ingredients in chess pie are eggs, sugar, vanilla, melted butter, vinegar, and cornmeal. My family's recipe is probably over 100 years old. I simply substituted the Bertolli Light olive oil for the cup of melted butter that the original recipe calls for, and added what I know to be ingredients used often in Italian cooking. Don't be "put off" by the cornmeal and the vinegar—the pie is wonderful!! And, with the use of Bertolli Light, a lot healthier!!

| | |
|---|---|
| ½ cup sliced almonds | ¼ cup almond oil |
| ½ cup packed light | 1  tablespoon cider vinegar |
|    brown sugar | 2  tablespoons cornmeal |
| 1  cup granulated sugar | 2  teaspoons almond extract |
| 4  eggs | 1  teaspoon vanilla extract |
| ½ cup Bertolli Light olive oil | 1  pie pastry (recipe below) |

Lightly toast the almond slices in a 325-degree oven—watch closely, so they won't burn. Whisk together the sugars and the eggs. Add the next 6 ingredients and whisk to completely incorporate the oils. Stir in the almonds. Pour into an unbaked pastry-lined pie pan. Bake in a preheated 325-degree oven for 55 to 60 minutes. Serves 6 to 8.

***Note:*** If baking 2 or more pies at once, you need to cook them longer—60 to 70 minutes. Optional: Serve with a dollop of whipped cream—plain!

# One-Pan Butterscotch Chocolate Brownies

### *I adore these rich moist brownies.*

In an ovenproof skillet, melt 1½ sticks of butter. Add 1 box of light brown sugar. Remove from the heat and add 2 cups of flour sifted with 2 teaspoons of baking powder and mix well. Add 2 beaten eggs, ¼ teaspoon salt, and 1 teaspoon vanilla extract and mix very well. Finally, mix in 1 cup of chopped pecans and a 6-ounce package of chocolate chips. Put the skillet in a 350-degree oven and bake for 30 minutes. Yum Yum! The Best Butterscotch Chocolate Brownie — I promise!

# Decadent Delicious Fabulous Brownies

| | |
|---|---|
| 3 squares each of semisweet and unsweetened chocolate (6 squares total) | 1 teaspoon baking powder |
| | ¾ teaspoon salt |
| | 1 tablespoon vanilla extract |
| 3 sticks butter | 2 cups chopped pecans or |
| 6 eggs | almonds or hazelnuts |
| 2¼ cups sugar | (or a mix of all 3) |
| ¾ cup flour | powdered sugar |

Melt the chocolate and the butter together. Cream the eggs and sugar together. Sift the flour, baking powder, and salt together. Mix all the above together and add the vanilla and nuts. Put in a greased 12x18-inch pan. Bake at 350 degrees for 30 to 35 minutes. Let cool. Sprinkle with powdered sugar. Cut the brownies. Absolutely fabulous!

*I am a cook who bakes for special occasions. I never bake cookies except at Christmas. The recipes I use are the Original Toll House Cookie and the oatmeal raisin cookie recipe on the Quaker Oats box — not very inventive, but still good. I do bake bread from time to time — mostly for special dinner parties. And I do make my own pizza crust. I still bake the boys their favorite cake on each one's birthday. I bake pies and cakes for Thanksgiving.*

*These recipes were and still are some of my favorite things to bake for the special times that I do bake.*

**Notes**

# Lime Squares

*A new twist on an old favorite. Refreshing and sweet-tart.*

### Combine for the crust:

| | |
|---|---|
| 1 cup coconut | ½ cup sugar |
| 1 cup butter | 1½ cups flour |

Press this in the bottom of a 9x9-inch pan and bake for 15 or so minutes at 350 degrees.

### Combine for the filling:

| | |
|---|---|
| 3 limes, quartered | 1 tablespoon plus 1 teaspoon |
| 2¼ cups sugar | vanilla extract |
| 4 eggs | powdered sugar |
| ½ cup flour | toasted coconut |
| 1 teaspoon baking powder | |

Put all this in the processor and pulse until puréed. Pour this over the baked crust. Bake at 350 degrees for 20 to 25 minutes. Cut after cooling and sprinkle with powdered sugar and toasted coconut.

# Graham Cracker Squares

*This recipe was given to me by Gabrielle Jarvis in 1963!*

| | |
|---|---|
| 2 cups smashed graham crackers | 1 cup chopped pecans |
| 6 ounces chocolate chips | 1 can sweetened condensed milk |

Mix all together and put in a very well greased, foil-lined (grease the foil) 9x9-inch pan.

Bake at 325 degrees for 25 to 30 minutes. When done, lift the foil from the pan and cut the squares. Release the squares from the foil by peeling it back. These are gooey and good!

# Aunt Mamie's Oatmeal
## ∽ Cookies Recipe ∾

### *The only cookie in this book.*

1 cup white sugar
½ cup butter
2 eggs
½ cup buttermilk
2 cups flour

1 teaspoon each baking soda
   and vanilla extract
1 cup each raisins, rolled oats,
   and coconut

Cream the sugar and butter. Beat in the eggs and buttermilk. Sift the flour and baking soda into it. Add the rest and mix well. Drop by teaspoonfuls onto a cookie sheet. Bake at 375 degrees for 8 to 12 minutes or until done.

# ∽ "Dixy" Doughnuts ∾

### *Aunt Mamie used to fix these for Buck's mother, Anne, and her sister, Dot. They nicknamed them "Big Boy Sinkers" because, even though they were delicious, they were heavy!*

3 tablespoons butter
1 cup sugar
1 cup buttermilk
1 teaspoon vanilla extract
1 egg

1 pound flour
⅛ teaspoon salt
1 teaspoon each baking soda
   and baking powder

Cream butter and sugar. Add buttermilk, vanilla, and the egg; beat. Sift in the flour, salt, baking soda, and baking powder; mix all well. Drop by tablespoonfuls into very hot oil. When done, sprinkle with confectioners' sugar if desired.

*You might add 6 ounces of chocolate chips and/or chopped pecans.*

# ~ My Version Of Amaretto Pie ~

*I'm saving the best pie for last. This is my version of the best damn pie I have ever put in my mouth — The Amaretto Cream Pie from the Mt. Vernon Restaurant in Chattanooga, Tennessee.*

*I have been able to come pretty close to the original, and I also created a Sensational Trifle using the Amaretto Cream filling. This makes 2 pies.*

## For the crusts:

Crush enough Nabisco Pecan Sandies to have 2¹/₂ cups of crumbs. Mix the crumbs with ¹/₂ cup melted butter and ¹/₂ cup chopped pecans. Press this in 2 pie pans. Bake for 5 minutes in a 350-degree oven. Set aside.

## Ingredients for the pies:

| | |
|---|---|
| 5 cups whole milk | 10 tablespoons butter |
| 4 egg yolks | 3¹/₂ tablespoons cornstarch |
| ³/₄ cup sugar | 2 envelopes gelatin, dissolved in |
| 2 teaspoons each vanilla extract and almond extract | ¹/₄ cup water |
| | 4 cups heavy cream |

Mix together 1 cup milk, 4 egg yolks, sugar, and the vanilla and almond extracts. Beat lightly and set aside.

In a heavy saucepan, bring 4 cups milk and the butter to the boil. Immediately reduce the heat to medium. Stir a small amount of the hot milk with the cornstarch and pour back into the hot milk; stir well. Put a small amount of the hot milk in the egg mixture to temper it and stir this into the hot milk. Cook, stirring constantly, until the custard is thick — don't overcook. After it is thickened, remove from the heat and let cool. Refrigerate after cooling completely,

When the custard is cold, dissolve the gelatin in the ¹/₄ cup cold water and heat over very low heat so it will be liquid — not grainy. Whisk the gelatin into the cold custard. Whip the cream to very stiff. Fold 2 cups of the whipped cream into the custard and put this into the pie shells.

Spread the remaining whipped cream on the top of the pies and refrigerate.

# ⇌ Sensational Trifle ⇋

Prepare the custard as described in Amaretto Pie up to folding in the whipped cream. Then take a tall, clear glass bowl and layer

1. Angel food cake pieces

2. Crushed Pecan Sandies

3. Half the custard

4. More cake pieces

5. More crumbs

6. The remaining custard

7. A generous layer of chopped pecans

8. 2 cups whipped cream

Chill thoroughly. Spoon into bowls—be sure to scoop through all the layers.

# ⇌ Menu ⇋

*I first served this at a holiday dinner
party we had in December 1995.*

Roasted Beef Tenderloin

Fettucine Alfredo

marinated blanched vegetables
in radicchio cups

2 loaves of Country Bread

Sensational Trifle

**Notes**

## ~ The Pickles ~

I am a driven person. I have a tendency to get completely immersed in projects — some say I become obsessed! This happened when I first decided that I would try my hand at pickling and preserving. I really came up with what I thought was the best way to do dill pickling and I began to dill pickle every imaginable vegetable in the world. I tried asparagus, green beans, fresh mushrooms, carrots, green tomatoes, okra, squash, both yellow and zucchini, fresh mild and hot chiles, along with cucumbers.

I think I processed over 50 jars of pickles in 2 or 3 days! That might be considered being obsessed by some, but to me it was fun — sort of a learning venture — a learning adventure at the least! Anyway, I thought I would try and pickle some Vidalia onions — Daddy had sent me about 30 pounds of them, and I had to come up with something to do with all those onions!

I love Vidalia onions. Like me, they also come from Georgia and they are uniquely sweet — I'm just kidding! Believe it or not, they were really great! One of the jars (there were 20 of them) went to some friends in Greenville, South Carolina. I didn't know at the time that they were acquainted with the president of Cate's Pickles. They contacted him about my pickled onion and I sent him a jar and the recipe.

To make a long story short, he thought they were delicious, but thought it wouldn't be cost effective to produce them in large quantities. So, the only dilled Vidalia that I have ever heard about would remain mine.

*Here are some assorted things that didn't quite "fit" anywhere else in the book!*

# ❧ Dilled Vidalias And Other Vegetables ❧

The processing is the same for all of the things that I pickle. Wash the vegetables.

| Whole and unpeeled: | Strips or ¼-inch slices unpeeled: | Peeled and sliced: |
|---|---|---|
| asparagus | | carrots |
| green beans | yellow squash | onions (Blanch |
| okra | zucchini | ¹/₂-inch slices in |
| green tomatoes | Kirby cucumbers | boiling water for 2 |
| chiles (mild or hot) | | minutes before |
| Kirby cucumbers | | placing in jars) |
| mushrooms | | |

Clean and sterilize quart canning jars and caps and seals.

Place in the bottom of each jar the following: 1 teaspoon mustard seeds, 2 teaspoons dill seeds, ¹/₂ teaspoon peppercorns, ¹/₄ teaspoon celery seeds, and 6 whole cloves of garlic. Place prepared vegetables of your choice in the jars.

In a large stockpot, bring 1 gallon white vinegar, 1¹/₂ gallons of water, and 1 cup of salt to the boil. When boiling, ladle this in the jars, leaving ¹/₄ inch of airspace at the top of the jar. Place the caps and seals on top after wiping the mouth of the jars. Screw down tight.

Keep in a cool place for 4 to 6 weeks before eating — refrigerate after opening.

# The Secret Of My Famous ❧ Green Pepper Jelly ❧

### *It's finally out! And you're the first to know!*

First, sterilize five or six ¹/₂-pint jelly jars and their caps and lids.

Cut 7 bell peppers into quarters. Put them in a large stockpot with 6 tablespoons crushed red pepper flakes, 1¹/₂ cups cider vinegar, and 6¹/₂ cups sugar. Bring this to the boil and cook for 3 or 4 minutes. Add 2 envelopes Certo Liquid and let this boil for 1 minute. Immediately pour into a colander that you have lined with cheesecloth or (and this is what I did and do) an old undershirt. Be sure it's clean and has no screening or printing on the part you strain the jelly through!! The colander should be over a large pot in your sink when you do this. Remove the colander and place the pot on the stove.

Add 5 or 6 drops green food coloring, bring back to the boil again, and immediately take off the stove. Very carefully ladle the jelly into five or six ¹/₂-pint jelly jars. Seal with tops and screw tight. You will have a clear, beautiful jelly.

## Notes ❧

*Try the dilled veggies instead of celery to garnish a Bloody Mary!!*

### *Shopping List*

*Vegetables of choice*
*Mustard seed*
*Dill seeds*
*Peppercorns*
*Celery seeds*
*Garlic*
*White vinegar*
*Salt*

## Notes

*Don't forget to sterilize the jars and lids.*

# Aunt Mamie's
# Watermelon Rind Preserves
### *A truly Southern thing.*

Peel the skin off the watermelon rind and cut away any of the red pulp. Mix the rind pieces with the same amount of sugar—for instance, 10 cups watermelon rind and 10 cups sugar. Let this stand overnight and then add 10 tablespoons full of orange peel. Put this, in batches, in the food chopper (I use the processor) and mince. Cook over medium-high heat until the rind is a rich yellow and the preserves are thick. Put in jars and seal. Store in a cool place.

# Iva Hussung's Never Store-Bought
# Homemade Mincemeat

| | |
|---|---|
| 2 pounds lean beef round | 5 pounds apples, cored and peeled |
| 1 pound suet | ¼ pound citron |

Boil the meat and let cool. Grind the meat, suet, apples, and citron.

Then add:

| | |
|---|---|
| 1 pound raisins | 1½ teaspoons cinnamon |
| 2 pounds currants | 1 teaspoon nutmeg |
| 1 quart apple juice | 1 tablespoon each mace, ground |
| 2½ pounds dark brown sugar | cloves, allspice, and salt |

Stir all of this together and put in pint freezer containers and freeze.

When ready to make pies, thaw and put in a pie shell. Top with pie pastry and bake at 325 degrees for 50 to 60 minutes.

One pint makes 1 pie.

# ~≪ Ann's Bloody Mary Mix ≫~

***This is the perfect mix to use for a crowd—for individual Bloodys, try Buck's Fish Bowl recipe.***

**Mix together:**

1 (14-ounce) bottle ketchup
1 (14-ounce) bottle Collins mix (can use frozen or powdered but reconstitute and then measure)
2 dashes of bitters
4 dashes of Tabasco sauce or to suit your taste

4 generous tablespoons horseradish
2 (46-ounce) cans of tomato juice
¼ cup red wine vinegar
¼ cup lemon juice

# ~≪ Buck's Fish Bowl Bloody Marys ≫~

Buck makes these special drinks in 24-ounce brandy snifters, however the recipe can be divided in half after it's made and put into two 12-ounce highball glasses before the ice is added.

For each drink:

6 ounces Tabasco Bloody Mary Mix
6 ounces Clamato Juice
1 teaspoon horseradish

1 dash Lea & Perrins Worcestershire sauce
3 dashes Tabasco sauce
¼ of a whole lime
freshly ground pepper

Mix all in the glass. Add 3 ounces Vodka (we use Skyy or Smirnoff) and stir. Now add the ice.

Garnish with a piece of celery or one of my dilled asparagus spears or my dilled green beans. You could use one of my dilled pickle spears. You could even use "store-bought"!!

***Note:*** Never add ice until a mixed drink is stirred!!

*This is the Bloody Mary recipe that the Atlanta Country Club uses to make their Bloody Marys. John Henderson's sister, Ann Henderson Weller, was able to talk the head bartender into giving it to her. Hooray for Ann!*

## Notes

*Joe Pryor is the Martini Master! He and Carol Ann explored Europe almost 3 weeks before they met us in Milan. They were in Scotland, Germany, and Switzerland. No one anywhere knew how to make a Martini! When he ordered one, he would invariably get a glass of Martini and Rossi dry Vermouth—not the Martini he had ordered. There are two versions—one for Vodka, and one for Gin.*

# Dr. Joe's Marvelous, Mellow Martinis

***Joe uses Ketel One Vodka and Bombay Gin. These he keeps in the freezer. The Vermouth should be kept in the refrigerator. His recipe will make enough to fill 2 glasses. If more are desired, pour out the ice and start over—each batch should be fresh.***

### Vodka Martini

To make Joe's Vodka Martini, wash the ice cubes and place them in a pitcher.

Now, put 4 jiggers of Ketel One Vodka in the pitcher and $1/4$ teaspoon of Vermouth—this amount will just barely cover the top of the Vermouth cap if you pour the Vermouth into the cap to measure it. Stir vigorously and pour into Martini glasses.

Put 1 or 2 queen-size olives in the Martini after you rinse them—or, cut a twist of lemon and add it.

To cut a twist: Cut the ends from the lemon, then make 2 vertical cuts into the lemon peel, $1/4$ inch apart, cutting through the peel but not the flesh. Pry the strip you have cut away from the lemon and twist the peel before putting it in the martini. Some people rub the peel around the edge of the glass before putting it in the glass.

### Gin Martini

To make Joe's Gin Martini, wash the ice and put in a pitcher.

Put 4 jiggers Bombay Gin in the pitcher and 1 jigger water and 1 jigger Vermouth. Stir vigorously and pour into Martini glasses.

Put in 2 rinsed olives or a lemon twist and enjoy!!

# Notes

# Notes

# Notes

# Notes

# Notes

# Notes

# Notes

# *Wise Words from Peggy*

Always rinse any ground beef under hot running water after it is cooked, and before adding to any recipe, to remove the unwanted extra grease. This extra grease is never needed and the rinsed ground beef will absorb the flavors of the dish better.

⌐——◆——⌐

Always add a little bit of sugar, about $^1/_2$ teaspoon, to any tomato-based dish—this will help reduce any acidity.

⌐——◆——⌐

Chew on a wooden match stick when chopping onions— you won't cry.

⌐——◆——⌐

To break the "seven years of bad luck" when you break a mirror, bury the mirror pieces with the mirror side down in a 7-inch hole in your backyard.

⌐——◆——⌐

To treat a dog that has "mange," dip it in a drum of crankcase oil— hold the front legs and dip up to its neck. Then rub the head and front legs with oil, and run, 'cause it's gonna shake that oil all over you and everything that's near!

# Index

**Notes**

**Notes**

**Notes**

**Notes**

Remember to Enjoy...
And have Fun !!!
Bye-Bye... for now...
See you again soon !


Love,

Robert

February 1997

# Order Information

| | Quantity | | | Total |
|---|---|---|---|---|
| *Pigs is Pigs and Folks is Folks* | _____ | X $16.95 | = | $ _____ |
| Tennessee residents add 8.25 % Sales Tax | | | = | $ _____ |
| Postage and Handling $3.50 each | | | = | $ _____ |
| | **TOTAL** | | = | $ _____ |

**RMH Enterprises**

**2969 Armory Drive, Suite 100A
Nashville, Tennessee 37204**

**Phone (615) 256-2100
Fax (615) 256-2121**

Name _____

Street Address _____

City _____ State _____ Zip _____

Daytime Phone ( ) ___ Nightime Phone ( ) ___

Method of Payment ☐ VISA ☐ MasterCard ☐ Check or Money Order

Card Number _____ Expiration Date _____

Signature _____

Please make check payable to RMH Enterprises.

*This form may be photocopied.*

---

| | Quantity | | | Total |
|---|---|---|---|---|
| *Pigs is Pigs and Folks is Folks* | _____ | X $16.95 | = | $ _____ |
| Tennessee residents add 8.25 % Sales Tax | | | = | $ _____ |
| Postage and Handling $3.50 each | | | = | $ _____ |
| | **TOTAL** | | = | $ _____ |

**RMH Enterprises**

**2969 Armory Drive, Suite 100A
Nashville, Tennessee 37204**

**Phone (615) 256-2100
Fax (615) 256-2121**

Name _____

Street Address _____

City _____ State _____ Zip _____

Daytime Phone ( ) ___ Nightime Phone ( ) ___

Method of Payment ☐ VISA ☐ MasterCard ☐ Check or Money Order

Card Number _____ Expiration Date _____

Signature _____

Please make check payable to RMH Enterprises.

*This form may be photocopied.*